ECCLESIASTICAL CENSURE AT THE
END OF THE FIFTEENTH CENTURY

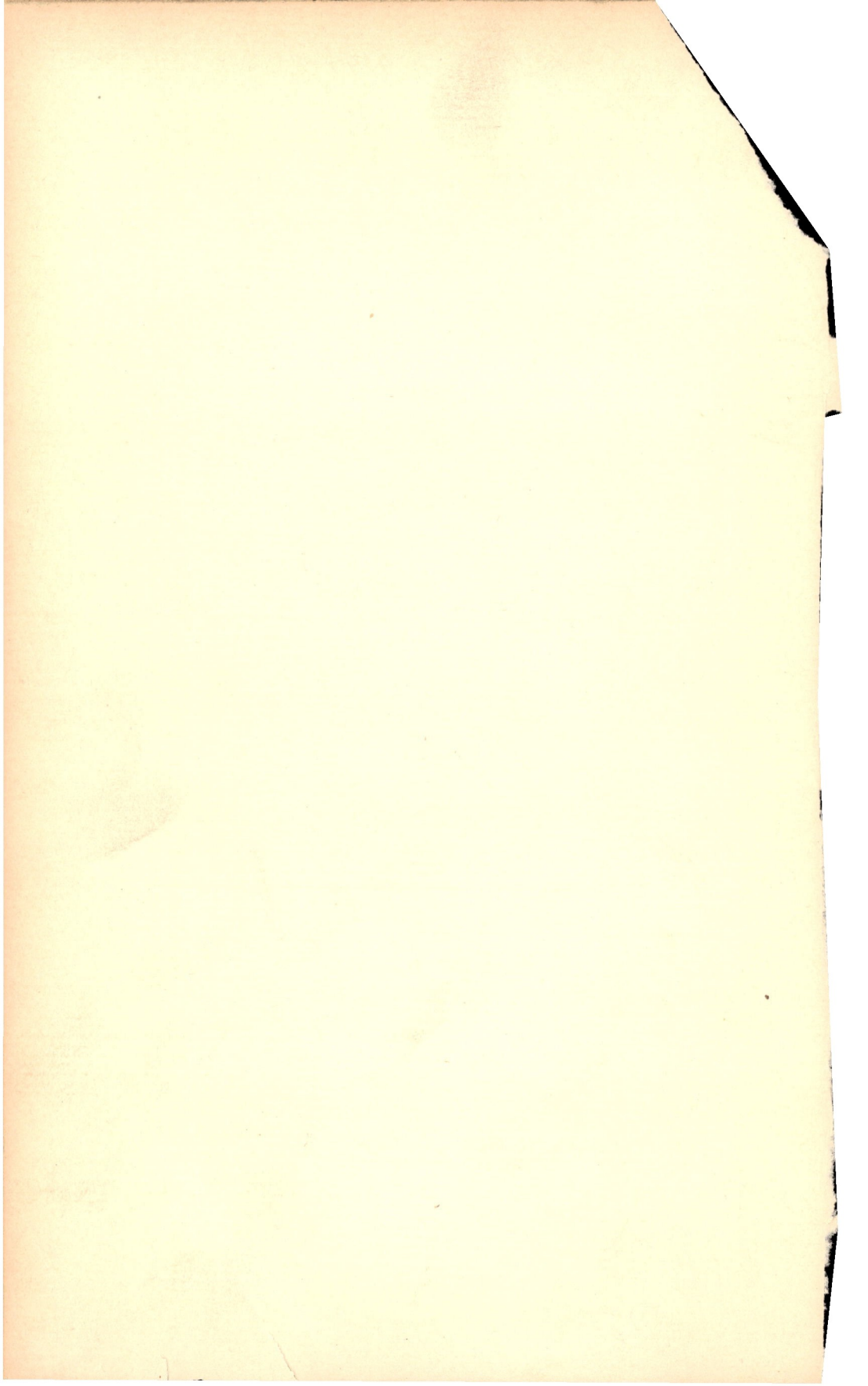

SERIES XLV   No. 3

JOHNS HOPKINS UNIVERSITY STUDIES

IN

HISTORICAL AND POLITICAL SCIENCE

Under the Direction of the

Departments of History, Political Economy, and
Political Science

———————

ECCLESIASTICAL CENSURE AT THE END OF THE FIFTEENTH CENTURY

BY

WILLIAM KURTZ GOTWALD, PH. D.
Assistant Professor of History, Wittenberg College

BALTIMORE
THE JOHNS HOPKINS PRESS
1927

J. H. FURST CO., PRINTERS, BALTIMORE

PREFACE

My interest in the history of the Reformation led me to make this particular study. It seemed profitable to study conditions in the period just preceding 1517, out of which the Reformation developed. I want to express here my deep gratitude to Professor John Martin Vincent, now Professor Emeritus of European History in the Johns Hopkins University, for his useful counsel and aid through criticisms and suggestions during the entire progress of the work. I owe him a debt which no mere line in a preface can repay.

W. K. G.

CONTENTS

ECCLESIASTICAL CENSURE AT THE END OF THE FIFTEENTH CENTURY

INTRODUCTION

The Papal Bull, Exsurge Domine, which was published June 15, 1520, condemned forty-one propositions drawn from the writings of Martin Luther, forbade the reading of his books, and called upon Christians everywhere to burn them. It threatened with excommunication every one who should support or protect him, suspended him from the priesthood, and announced his excommunication if he did not repent or recant within sixty days after the publication of the Bull in Germany. An interdict was laid, also, on any place where Luther should be, and for three days after he left.

The Bull led a checkered career in Germany, ending with its dramatic burning by Luther, outside the wall of Wittenberg.

The question arises as to the relative importance of this incident. Were excommunications and interdicts frequent at this time? What and how great effects did they have? What was the opinion generally held concerning them? Krehbiel has made an excellent study of this, covering the twelfth and thirteenth centuries, at the height of the power of the Mediaeval Church. It is the purpose of the present study to attempt to answer these questions concerning the latter half of the fifteenth century and the opening of the sixteenth— roughly speaking, from 1450 to 1517. This period has been chosen, first, because by a comparison with conditions in the earlier period, the development of the use of ecclesiastical censures can be shown; second, because of its connection with the excommunication of Luther, as indicated above; and third, because a period of this length can be more easily studied.

But this latter half of the fifteenth century is interesting

1

for itself. During this period the humanism of the Renaissance seized hold of the Papacy. In 1449 the Council of Basel, the last of the Reforming Councils, had closed—or rather, broken up. It had reaffirmed the decrees of Constance subordinating all ecclesiastical authority to that of a general council. For a while, Pope Eugene had acknowledged their claims, but later had repudiated them. He then dissolved the Council, which, in its turn, deposed him. The Pope, however, won Germany to his support from that of the Council, and upon his death in 1447 the Council recognized his successor, Nicholas V, and decreed its own dissolution.

There then began a Papal reaction—Pius II, who before his accession was Aeneas Sylvius, a leading humanist, used, as we shall see, the excommunication as a weapon in forwarding this reaction. Under Sixtus IV (1471-1484) the Papacy sank to the level of the contending principalities which surrounded it. Sixtus, in carrying out his program of vigorous secular activity, needed, first of all, assistants in whom he could place confidence. He, therefore, made nepotism a political principle and placed his relatives in the most prominent positions. The pontificate of Innocent VIII (1484-1492) was an interval of indolent and aimless drifting in which the general immorality of the time became more pronounced than ever. The policy of political activity was continued by Alexander VI (1492-1503), a handsome and sensual man, who while still a Cardinal had made his Catalan kinsmen all-powerful in Rome. The Papacy was now more absolute than ever before in ecclesiastical matters. Its world-wide financial system gave it the appearance of being a great financial institution, and its activity in diplomacy and warfare stamped it as a political power. At the death of Alexander, followed Pius III, with a pontificate of less than a month. Then followed the martial Julius II (1503-1513), who was determined to make the Papal State the strongest in Italy. He was succeeded by Leo X, the second son of Lorenzo de Medici, a most magnificent patron of the Renaissance.

In France, during this period, the kingdom was being consolidated and the power centralized in the hands of the king. This task was pursued by Louis XI (1461-1483) who was aided by a permanent royal army and a permanent special tax for its support, established by his predecessor, Charles VII. He was succeeded by his son, Charles VIII (1483-1498), a lad of fourteen, whose mind was filled with the legends of chivalry. For the first half of his reign his older sister, Anne of Beaujeu, was the regent of France. The marriage of the young king to Anne of Brittany resulted eventually in the annexation to the crown of that last of the great feudatory states of France. The country became more prosperous than ever before; and Charles, after becoming free from the restraint of his sister Anne, began to look to the fulfillment of his dreams of conquest. Through the house of Anjou, whose rights had descended to him, Charles had a claim to Naples, and his cousin and brother-in-law had a claim to Milan. In 1494, Charles recrossed the Alps with the purpose of conquering Naples. On through Piacenza, Florence, Siena, Rome, and to Naples he went. It was an easy victory. But at Venice, March 31, 1495, was formed a league between Germany, Spain, Milan, the Papacy, and Venice, whose purpose was to expel the French from Naples. Charles retreated northward, got the better of the Milanese and Venetian troops at Fornovo, though he was greatly outnumbered, and evacuated Italy.

Louis XII (1498-1515) succeeded to the French throne and united in his own person the French claims upon Milan and Naples. He immediately began preparations for a second invasion of Italy. The Venetian league dissolved, since its Italian members were jealous of each other. The Pope desired a powerful ally, and Venice wished for the downfall of Milan. Milan was conquered by the French, and Louis then turned his attention to the South. In 1500 a secret treaty was concluded at Granada for a combined conquest of Naples by France and Aragon, and a division of the territory, which agreement was confirmed by the Pope. In 1504, however, Louis was obliged to resign Naples to King Ferdinand of Aragon, while with regard to Milan, the conflict continued with varying fortunes.

The commerce of the Middle Ages had stimulated the growth of important trading towns in Italy, in Germany and in the Netherlands. These towns, in one way or another, managed to secure a large measure of self-government, so that by the end of the fifteenth century they had become similar to the city-states of the Greeks and Romans. In the case of Italy, it is impossible to understand this period without paying considerable attention to these city-states, for in the Italy of the end of the fifteenth century there was no semblance of national unity. Despite the ardent longings of many Italian patriots, and the use of a common language, which, under such writers as Dante and Petrarch, had become a great medium for literary expression, the people of Italy had not built up a national monarchy. The peninsula could be divided geographically into the city-states of the north, the Papal States, and the kingdom of Naples. Of these, the ancient kingdom of Naples comprised the southern third of the peninsula. This, with the Island of Sicily, comprised the kingdom of the Two Sicilies. In 1442 this kingdom was united under the rule of the house of Aragon—though this claim, as we have seen, was not allowed by the King of France until 1504. Socially and politically, Naples was the most backward state in Italy.

About the city of Rome had grown up, in the course of centuries, the Papal States, or, as they were officially styled, the Patrimony of St. Peter. It had early fallen to the bishop, as the most important person in the city, to exercise political power in Rome during the barbarian invasions. The Pope had slowly extended his territories through central Italy from the Tiber to the Adriatic, which, at the end of the fifteenth century, as we have seen, had sunk to the level of the surrounding Italian States.

North and west of the Papal States were the various city-states. These towns had reached a higher plane, both of material prosperity and intellectual culture, than was to be found at that time in any other part of Europe. They were, however, deeply jealous of each other and carried on an interminable series of petty wars, using professional hired soldiers, headed by captains, or condottieri. The most famous of these city-states were Milan, Venice, Genoa, and Florence.

Of these cities, Milan was in theory a ducal fief of the Holy Roman Empire, but had long been in fact the prize of despotic rulers who were descended from two famous families—the Visconti and the Sforza—and who combined the patronage of art with the politics of Italian tyrants. The Visconti ruled Milan from the thirteenth century until the middle of the fifteenth, when a Sforza, one of the condottieri, established the supremacy of his own family. In 1499, as we have seen, Louis XII of France, claiming the duchy as heir to the Visconti, seized Milan.

Venice was the type of the commercial oligarchical city-states, and was by far the most powerful state in the peninsula. Located on the islands and lagoons at the head of the Adriatic, she had profited greatly by the crusades to build up a maritime empire and an enviable trade on the eastern Mediterranean, and had extended her sway over rich lands in the northeastern part of Italy. Venice boasted of 3,000 ships, 300,000 sailors, a numerous and veteran army, famous factories of plate glass, silk stuffs and gold and silver objects. We shall find two excommunications hurled against her by two different Popes during this period, and we shall see her interfere with regard to other excommunicated persons and States, in a way which shows the great independence of her religious feeling.

Nominally, Venice was a republic—actually, an oligarchy. Political power was entrusted jointly to several agencies: a grand council controlled by the commercial magnates; a centralized committee of ten; an elected doge, or duke; and, after 1454, three state inquisitors, henceforth the city's masters. The inquisitors could pronounce sentence of death, dispose of the public funds, and enact statutes; they maintained a regular spy system, and trial, judgment, and execution were secret. To this regime Venice owed the internal peace which contrasted with the endless civil wars of the other Italian cities.

In foreign affairs, Venice possessed a considerable influence. She was the first European state to send envoys, or ambassadors, to other courts; and the reports of these ambassadors give us colorful pictures of the politics and life of the several states during this period. Already, however, the seeds of her downfall had been sown. The advance of the Ottoman Empire threatened her position in eastern Europe, though she still held the Morea in Greece, Crete, Cyprus, and many Aegean islands. The discovery of America and of a new route to India was to shake the very basis of her commercial supremacy. Her unscrupulous policy towards her Italian rivals lost her friends in the west. Indeed, because of this great enmity, the emperor, the Pope Julius II, France, and Spain entered into the formidable League of Cambrai, in 1508, to crush her, the Pope agreeing to use spiritual as well as temporal arms against her. So also Genoa, second only to Venice in commercial importance, passed through all kinds of political vicissitudes, until she fell prey to the invasion of Louis XII of France, in 1499.

Florence may be taken as the best type of the democratic community, controlled by a political leader. The city, famous for its free institutions and for its art, had come, in the first half of the fifteenth century, under the tutelage of a rich family of traders and bankers, the Medici, who preserved the republican forms, and for a while under Lorenzo de Medici (1449-1492) surnamed the Magnificent, made Florence the center of Italian culture and civilization. We shall see the reaction of Lorenzo, and of Florence in his time, toward excommunication and interdict. Soon after his death, a democratic movement took place under the monk Savonarola, who welcomed the advent of Charles VIII of France and aided in the expulsion of the Medici. Savonarola was put to death in 1498. The democracy managed to survive until 1512, when the Medici returned.

The city-state was the dominant form of political organization also in the Netherlands. The Netherlands, or Low

Countries, were seventeen provinces occupying the flat low-lands along the North Sea—the territory which is now Holland, Belgium, and northern France. Most of the inhabitants, Flemish and Dutch, spoke a language akin to German, but in the south the Walloons used a French dialect. Gradually, in the course of the twelfth to the fourteenth centuries, important towns had arisen, so wealthy and populous that they were able to wrest charters from their lords. Thus had arisen a number of municipalities—practically self-governing republics—semi-independent vassals of feudal nobles; and in many cases the early oligarchic systems of municipal government had given way to more democratic institutions. Remarkable in industry and prosperity were Ghent, Bruges, Antwerp, Brussels, Liège, Utrecht, Delft, and Rotterdam.

Gradually, throughout the fourteenth and fifteenth centuries, the dukes of Burgundy, who, as vassals of the French king had long held the duchy of that name in eastern France, succeeded by marriage, purchase, treachery or force, in bringing one by one the seventeen provinces of the Netherlands under their rule. In 1465 a common parliament, called the States General, was constituted at Brussels containing deputies from each of the seventeen provinces; and in 1473, a grand council. Charles the Bold, who died in 1477, was prevented from constructing a great central kingdom between France and the Germanies only by the shrewdness of his foe, Louis XI of France. Louis seized the duchy of Burgundy, on the death of Charles, thus extending the eastern frontier of France, but the duke's inheritance in the Netherlands passed to his daughter Mary. Mary married Maximilian of Austria in 1477, and we shall see a pope interfering with excommunication on Maximilian's side, in his quarrels with his subjects.

In central Europe, survived, in weakness, at the end of the fifteenth century, an empire. The theory of an empire was a very ancient one—it meant a state which should embrace all peoples of whatsoever race or language, bound together in obedience to a common prince. Such had been the ideal of the old Roman Empire, under whose Caesars practically the whole civilized world had been joined. A thousand years before the fifteenth century it had lost control of the West because of external violence and internal weakness. So great, however, was the strength of an "empire" even in the West, that Charlemagne, about the year 800, had temporarily united what are now called France, Germany, Italy, the Netherlands, and Belgium, into what he styled the "Roman Empire." Nearly two centuries later Otto the Great, a German prince, gave another form to the idea, in the "Holy Roman Empire" of which he became emperor. This form continued from 962 to 1806.

By the end of the fifteenth century, however, the Holy Roman Empire was practically restricted to German-speaking peoples. The papacy and the Italian cities had been freed from imperial control, and both the Netherlands, that is, Holland and Belgium, and the Swiss cantons were only nominally connected. Over the Slavic peoples to the East—Russians, Poles, and others—or the Scandinavians to the north, the empire had comparatively small influence. Yet the King of Bohemia was one of the seven "electors" who chose the Emperor. However, the words "Empire" and "Germany" had become virtually interchangeable terms. Moreover, throughout central Europe there was no conspicuous desire for strong centralized national states—separatism was the rule. Within the Holy Roman Empire was a vast mixture of city-states, and feudal survivals—arch-duchies, such as Austria; margravates such as Württemberg; counties, like the Palatinate; and a host of free cities, baronies and domains. In all, there were over three hundred states which collectively were called "the Germanies" and were united by the imperial tie.

The Holy Roman Empire had the form of a central government with an emperor to execute laws and a Diet to make them. The emperor was not necessarily hereditary, but was chosen by seven "electors," who were the chief princes of the realm. These seven were the archbishops of Mainz, of Cologne, and of Trier; the King of Bohemia; the duke of Saxony; the margrave of Brandenburg; and the count palatine of the Rhine. We shall see an archbishop of Mainz excommunicated, and a series of excommunications and interdicts arising out of the charge of heresy against a King of Bohemia. Not infrequently the electors used their position to extort concessions from the emperor-elect, which helped to destroy German unity and to promote the selfish interests of the princes. The imperial Diet was composed of the seven electors, the lesser princes, including the higher ecclesiastical dignitaries, such as bishops and abbots; and representatives of the free cities; grouped in three separate houses. The emperor was not supposed to perform any imperial act without the authorization of the Diet, and petty jealousies between its members often prevented action in the Diet. The individual states, moreover, reserved to themselves the management of very many affairs. The Diet, and therefore the emperor, was without a treasury or an army, unless the individual states saw fit to act favorably upon its advice and furnish the requested quotas. It resembled far more a congress of diplomats than a legislative body.

Signs were not wanting of some national life in the Germanies. Most of the people spoke a common language, a form of national unity existed in the Diet; and many patriots raised their voice in behalf of a stronger and more centralized government. We shall see manifestations of this national feeling in the course of this study. In 1495, a Diet met at the city of Worms to discuss with the Emperor Maximilian projects of reform. After protracted debates, it was agreed that private warfare, a survival of feudal days, should be abolished; a perpetual peace should be declared; and an imperial court should be established to settle all disputes between states within the empire. These efforts at reform were, however, unfruitful.

The Bohemians, despite the fact that their kings received investiture from the German emperor, and were included among the seven electors, had been drawn together by the struggles of the Hussite movement. The national spirit of the Bohemians, or Czechs, had been stimulated and in 1409 the German element had been expelled from the University

2

of Prague. The most influential spokesman of this revival of national feeling had been John Hus, a teacher and a priest. From Wiclif and from Bohemian thinkers he had inherited heretical views. On July 6, 1415, he had been burned at the stake, at Constance, where he had been induced under a guarantee of safety, to attend the general council. The treacherous death of the popular leader had kindled a terrible war. This Bohemian revolt had been distinctly national in character, and all classes of society had participated in it. The insurgents, inspired by fanaticism and aided by the strategic skill of John Ziska, burning churches and monasteries, had swept over Bohemia. In this revolt there were interwoven an insurrection against the authority of the Church, an outbreak of national spirit, and an attempt to settle the fundamental problems that confront secular society. We shall find a series of excommunications and interdicts in connection with the heresy of King George of Bohemia, who died in 1472.

In 1453, the Hundred Years' War ended, leaving to England on the continent only the town of Calais. The kingdom of Scotland still preserved an independence, while Irish princes and chieftains rendered English occupation of their island extremely precarious beyond the Pale of Dublin. The outcome of the Hundred Years' War served to exalt the sense of English nationality and English patriotism, and to enable the king to devote his whole attention to the consolidation of his power in the British islands. For several years after the conclusion of peace on the Continent, England was harassed by bloody and confused struggles known as the Wars of the Roses, between rival claimants to the throne, but in 1485 Henry VII (1485-1509), the first of the Tudor dynasty, secured the crown and ushered in a new era of English history. Henry sought to create what has been termed a " strong monarchy." The Wars of the Roses had two effects which were to the advantage of the king; the struggle, really a contest of two factions of nobles, destroyed many noble families and enabled the crown to seize their estates, thereby lessening the influence of an ancient class.

It also created in the middle class or "common people" a longing for peace and the conviction that order and security could be maintained only by repression of the nobility and the strengthening of monarchy.

Henry took advantage of these circumstances to fix upon his country absolutism, or one-man power in government. We shall find the Popes assisting him in this with the excommunication, and we shall find him holding a very high opinion of this spiritual weapon. He repressed disorder with a heavy hand and secured the establishment of an extraordinary court to hear cases, especially those affecting the nobles, which the ordinary courts had not been able to settle. He was also very economical: the public revenue was increased by means of more careful attention to the cultivation of the crown lands and the collection of feudal dues, fines, benevolences, import and export duties, and past parliamentary grants, while, by means of frugality and a foreign policy of peace, the expenditure was decreased. Henry was therefore freed in large measure from dependence on Parliament for grants of money, and the power of Parliament declined. In fact, it met only five times during the whole reign, and only once during the last twelve years, and in all its actions was quite subservient to the king's desires.

This study is an assemblage and examination of the outstanding instances of ecclesiastical censure which occurred within a limited period and were cases well known to the public and likely to exert a wide influence. It exhibits the extent of the power of the Church when in conflict with civil authorities, and, incidentally, the effect on the popular mind. The citation of cases from France, Germany, Florence, Venice, England, Bohemia, and other states, all falling within the half century preceding the Reformation, will give, it is hoped, by this very accumulation, some additional understanding of the strength of opposing forces in the conflict.

CHAPTER I

Use of Censures During the Papal Reaction After 1450

The two leaders in the Papal Reaction after 1450, Nicholas, Cardinal Cusa, and Pope Pius II, made frequent use of censures in carrying out their projects. Cusa, as Bishop of Brixen in the Tyrol, was interested in reform. The Poor Clares of Brixen would not accept his reforms and Cusa feared "lest he might incur censure by censuring insensate women or less reasonable animals." He did, however, lay an interdict upon them, January 15, 1455. They remained contumacious three or four months.[1] Cardinal Cusa had demanded of the nuns of the Benedictine Abbey of Sonnenburg, stricter observance of the closure, on threat of censure. In May, 1452, the monition was reported by the nuns to Duke Sigismund of Austria, asking him for protection. The Abbess Verena asked the Duke to intercede with the Cardinal to postpone the threatened penalty. The Councillors of the Duke therefore asked the Cardinal to postpone the penalty until he should return to the diocese,[2] and as a result the Cardinal allowed a postponement until St. Gall's Day.[3]

In June, 1454, the Cardinal laid an interdict on this convent.[4] The nuns appealed twice to the Pope and sent a copy of their appeal to the Archbishop of Salzburg. Their second appeal they also affixed to the doors of the Cathedral of Brixen. A priest of the diocese of Eichstadt, Andreas Mack, carried the appeal to Rome.[5] In April of the next year the Cardinal proceeded to excommunicate the Abbess and deprive her of her office, and the nuns immediately wrote to the Duchess Eleonore for help against the Cardinal.[6] The nuns, together with Elizabeth Ketzin, the dean, continued to

---

[1] G. Voigt, Piccolomini als Pabst Pius der Zweite und sein Zeitalter, vol. iii, p. 314; Archiv für Oesterreichische Geschichte, vol. iv, p. 305.

[2] Ibid., vol. vii, p. 152. [3] Ibid., p. 153.

[4] Ibid., p. 154. [5] Ibid., pp. 158, 159.

[6] Ibid., p. 160.

obey the Abbess in spite of the excommunication. For this reason the abbey was laid under interdict.[7] However, the peasants who were on the lands of the Sonnenburg Monastery refused to pay their rents because of the excommunication of the Abbess.[8] The nuns complained to Duke Sigismund of the strictness of the interdict. "Three hundred were left to die without confession and absolution."[9] In negotiations between Duke Sigismund and the Cardinal, in 1458, the Duke stipulated that the Abbess and the nuns should ask for absolution from excommunication. The Cardinal demanded that the Abbess be absolved in person, but this she refused to do, as it would be an act of dishonor.[10] The Abbess was finally absolved.[11]

In the meanwhile, Cusa and Duke Sigismund had quarreled and Cusa had been shut up in the Castle at Buchenstein. For this, Pope Calixtus III threatened Duke Sigismund and his subjects with excommunication and interdict "if he does not set Cardinal Cusa entirely free within eight days." In October he placed the Duke's territory under interdict.[12] The Duke protested to the Pope against the interdict. "He does not recognize the interdict out of honor to the Church. The interdict will dishonor the Church, especially if Cusa is in charge of it."[13] February 6, 1458, the Duke appealed a second time to the Pope "better informed" in the presence of representatives of the towns of Brixen and Bruneck and of the Cathedral Chapter, and a number of nobles. The same month, also, the parish clergy of the Duke's lands appealed in a gathering at Brixen against Cusa's threat to suspend *cura animorum* in Mid-Lent; and fixed their appeal to the Church doors at Brixen. In the meanwhile, Gerhard von Berlach, a member of the Chapter, read to the assembled clergy the regulations for the observ-

---

[7] Ibid., p. 165.
[8] Voigt, vol. iii, p. 339.
[9] Arch. für Oester. Gesch., vol. vii, p. 167.
[10] Voigt, vol. iii, p. 343; Arch. für Oester. Gesch., vol. vii, p. 170.
[11] Voigt, vol. iii, p. 345.
[12] Arch. für Oester. Gesch., vol. iv, pp. 310, 311.
[13] Ibid., vol. iv, p. 311.

ance of the interdict. Finally, April 12, Cusa laid Tyrol under the interdict, which, however, was observed in but few places. The Cardinal then permitted worthy priests to continue their offices until July 2, and he classed as worthy those who had observed the interdict, and had not signed the appeal.[14] On July 2, however, when the interdict was again declared in force, it was as little observed as before.[15]

At the Congress held by Pope Pius II, at Mantua, the Duke Herzog complained of the interdict laid by Cusa on the Tyrol " coming to the Pope, not as a child to its father, but as a Prince, demanding satisfaction for his wounded honor, and the righting of his wrongs." [16]   In February, 1460, Cusa again ordered the interdict, and on April 27 he had it observed at Bruneck, though many people had come up for a church feast. The following month, however, he complained to the parish priests at Brixen that the interdict was not observed.[17]   Pope Pius II then issued a Monitorium to Duke Sigismund and his followers, citing them to Rome the first Monday in August to answer for the imprisonment of Cardinal Cusa at Bruneck, on Easter Day.   July 14, Sigismund prepared an appeal, in the mildest form, to the Pope better informed. A great number of Abbots and parish priests signed, as adhering to this appeal, practically the entire diocese of Brixen, with the exception of the priests on the lands of the Count of Görz. Because of this appeal the Tyrolese priests failed to observe Cusa's interdict.[18]

The Pope issued a Bull on August 8, excommunicating Duke Sigismund and all who had helped him against the Cardinal, especially the inhabitants of the town and castle of Bruneck. All oaths, vows, or agreements made with them were declared void, and their goods were to be confiscated to the Apostolic Treasury. Their lands were placed under strictest interdict; the faithful were to cease all intercourse with them, to sell them nothing, and to buy nothing from them.

---

[14] Ibid., vol. iii, pp. 336, 337.
[15] Ibid., vol. iii, p. 339.   [16] Ibid., vol. iv, p. 318.
[17] Ibid., pp. 320, 322, 323.
[18] Ibid., p. 323; Voigt, vol. iii, pp. 366, 372.

With this general Bull of Excommunication the Pope issued an explanatory one, in which he named as excommunicates besides the Duke, about ten nobles, one hundred laymen, the Nuns of Sonnenburg, and one priest. He also directed a Brief to the clergy of the Brixen diocese in which he threatened trials for heresy for those who refused to observe the interdict.[19] Following this the Duke issued a new and sharper appeal:

> We appeal, therefore, to a future Pope who may revise the doings of his predecessor; further, to a General Council, to be held in accordance with the decrees of Constance and Basel. Nor is this appeal a subterfuge, as we do not wish to avoid the course of natural justice. As the Pope has rendered himself notoriously suspected, we will accept any impartial judge, whom he may name; we do not refuse his sentence as President of a General Council. If this be denied us, we appeal further, to the whole people of our Savior Jesus Christ; we appeal to all who love justice and favor innocency. If this be denied us, we call God to witness that it is not our fault, that justice is not done, that we are oppressed.

About a month later the Duke issued a second appeal to a future Pope or a future council. These appeals and the writings that followed he sent into all Germany.[20]

In defense of the Church against the excommunicated Sigismund the Pope called upon the Swiss, the Count of Görz, the Archbishop of Salzburg, the Bishop of Trent, the Doge of Venice, Duke Ludwig of Bavaria, and the Bishop of Wurzburg. He also sent the Bishop of Basel a threatening brief for disregarding the censures against Sigismund.[21] He attempted by threats and warning to cause the city of Augsburg to cease trading with the Tyrol. A friar appeared in the city and preached against Sigismund; some parish priests refused certain burghers absolution because they had sold goods in the markets of Meran and Botzen; but the chronicler (Annales Augsburgenses) considers these priests shameless men. The Council of Nuremberg informed the Pope that Duke Sigismund had not visited their city since

---

[19] M. Freher, vol. ii, p. 200 ff.; Voigt, vol. iii, p. 375; Arch. für Oester. Gesch., vol. iv, p. 325.

[20] M. Freher, vol. ii, p. 205 ff.; Arch. für Oester. Gesch., vol. iv, p. 326.

[21] Ibid., p. 324; Voigt, vol. iii, pp. 391, 396, 397.

the Excommunication, and that if their clergy would have observed the interdict, they would not have prevented it.[22] The Minorite Martin von Rottenburg was sent into the dioceses of Aquileia and Salzburg to preach on Sigismund's heresy. In March, 1461, he was in Salzburg, at Easter in Ratisbon, where, in spite of the objections of the town council, he published the Excommunication in the Cathedral; but his life was in danger.[23] The Poor Clares of Brixen strictly observed the interdict under the leadership of their father confessor, Brother Nicholas from Prussia.[24] Their church remained closed sixteen weeks, and neither singing nor the ringing of bells was heard in the cloister.

On the other hand, on September 21, 1460, the Cathedral Chapter protested against the interdict on the towns of Brixen and Bruneck. The King of France, the Doge of Venice, the Duke of Milan, the Electors of Mainz, Cologne, and Trier, Archduke Albert of Brandenburg, and Duke Ludwig of Bavaria, adhered to Sigismund's appeal of August 13. The Cardinal of Augsburg mentioned the excommunication of Sigismund among the grievances of the German nation against the Pope.[25] The Doge of Venice and the Duke of Milan forbade the publishing of Bulls against Sigismund, while the Doge expressed his sympathy with Sigismund and offered his help.[26] In spite of the excommunication, the Swiss entered into an armistice with Sigismund, at Costnitz, in December, preparatory to negotiations for peace. The parish priest of the diocese of Costnitz, also, failed to publish the censures. The Bishop of Basel entered the negotiations for peace, in spite of the Pope's warning that in so doing he would come under the censures against Sigismund. The Cardinal of Augsburg set the example for the Bishops in Bavaria and Suabia by allowing the export of salt and wine into the Tyrol.[27]

---

[22] Ibid., p. 398.
[23] Arch. für Oester. Gesch., vol. vii, p. 175; Voigt, vol. iii, p. 399.
[24] Ibid., pp. 400, 401.
[25] Ibid., pp. 391, 393; H. C. Senckenberg, Selecta juris et historiarum, vol. iv, p. 390.
[26] Arch. für Oester. Gesch., vol. iv, p. 328; Voigt, vol. iii, 396, 397.
[27] Voigt, vol. iii, pp. 394, 396, 397.

In February, 1461, the Cathedral Chapter of Brixen had read from its pulpit the statement that there is no interdict on Brixen; that the Chapter has chartered right to conduct the cure of souls; that the interdict on Brixen has never been published; that the worship is continued, not in opposition to Pope or Bishop, but to the glory of God and the cure of souls.[28] Then two Franciscan monks came to Brixen to preach on the interdict. One of them, Martin Wela, was arrested, taken in chains to Innsbruck, and saved from drowning in the Inn only by the intervention of the Duke. The Bishop of Trent failed to observe the interdict, and made a treaty with the excommunicated Sigismund. The Archbishop of Salzburg kept the Bull of Excommunication secret for months while the appeal remained fixed to the cathedral doors.[29]

Pope Pius II, on January 23, 1461, summoned Sigismund to Rome to answer, within sixty days, for heresy because of his despising of the censures, together with his adherents. These were, the Bishop of Trent, who had been deposed; Gregory Heimburg and Lamentius Blumenau, Percival von Annenberg, and other councillors of the Duke; the inhabitants of Meran, Chur, Hall, Innsbruck and Sterzing, all subjects of Sigismund in the dioceses of Chur, Trent and Brixen, all the clergy and burghers of Brixen; and all who had not observed the interdict.[30] We may note here the apparent close connection between censures and heresy. The despising of the censures was heresy. The step from excommunication to a charge of heresy was a very short one.

In answer to this summons the Cathedral Chapter appealed on March 2, and Sigismund on the sixteenth. He answered the Pope's charge of despising censures by denying that he was bound by censures; what the Bull termed such were idle falsehoods.[31] Thereupon the Pope included Sigismund and

---

[28] Arch. für Oester. Gesch., vol. vii, p. 176.

[29] Voigt, vol. iii, pp. 400-402.

[30] Raynaldus, Annales Ecclesiastici, vol. x, anno 1461, No. 11; cf. Voigt, vol. iii, pp. 404, 405.

[31] Arch. für Oester. Gesch., vol. vii, p. 177; Voigt, vol. iii, pp. 406, 407.

his adherents in the Holy Thursday Bull of Excommunication. In July negotiations between the Pope and Sigismund were begun at Landshut, the Pope's conditions including the absolution of Sigismund after penance. Sigismund answered that he would suffer death first, as by absolution he would admit himself under censure.[32] The Doge of Venice attempted a reconciliation. On September 16, 1462, the Pope empowered the Bishop of Feltre to suspend the censures and interdict over Tyrol until the following January. But the Cathedral Chapter of Brixen protested against the proclamation of the suspension, since "here no censures lawful, or lawfully fulminated, exist." As a result, the Pope declared the censures again in full force, February, 1463.[33] Finally, owing to the influence of the Emperor Frederick III, the Emperor, in place of Sigismund, obtained absolution, in Wiener Neustadt, in the presence of the Papal Legate, and the interdict was at last removed from Sigismund's lands September 2, 1464.[34]

Diether, Archbishop of Mainz, failed to pay the Annates at his confirmation as Archbishop, and as a result, he was sentenced with lesser excommunication by "inferior judges . . . without the knowledge of the Pope," Pius II.[35] When he heard of this he "became so excited that he threatened to move heaven and earth. He . . . utterly disregarded this excommunication." [36] He appealed to a Council, and was supported in his appeal by the Count Palatine Frederick, the Elector Frederick of Brandenburg, with his brothers, Albert and John, and the Bishop of Würzburg. Efforts were made to win the city of Mainz for the appeal. Before deciding, however, Mainz asked advice on the matter from Frankfort.[37] In December, 1460, Diether, together with the

---

[32] Arch. für Oester. Gesch., vol. vii, p. 180.

[33] Ibid., vol. iii, p. 183; Voigt, vol. iii, pp. 416-417.

[34] Ibid., pp. 419, 420.

[35] Bull of Aug. 22, 1461, depriving Diether of his archbishopric (Raynaldus, vol. x, anno 1461, par. 21).

[36] Orig. Report of Bessarion, Papal Legate, to Pius II from Vienna, 1461 (L. von Pastor, Geschichte der Päpste seit dem Ausgang des Mittelalters, vol. iii, p. 174, Eng. Trans.).

[37] Senckenberg, vol. iv, pp. 392-399; G. C. Joannis, Scriptores rerum Mogunticarum, vol. i, p. 776; Pastor, vol. iii, p. 174, n. 5.

Pfalzgraf Frederick, arranged to support King George Podie-brad of Bohemia in his attempt to undertake to call a General Council, to be held in a Rhine city, to repeat and administer the Basel Decrees, especially those concerning Confirmations, Annates, and the jurisdiction of the Roman Court, and to take care that the Pope should claim from Diether no larger sum for the Pallium than was customary. Diether also called a Diet at Bamberg at which he presented a document appealing against all ecclesiastical censures. The representative of the Electors of Brandenburg and Saxony, and the King of Bohemia refused to sign it. It was said that the clergy of Mainz did not adhere to the Archbishop's appeal. The Elector Frederick of Saxony, May 11, 1461, instructed his representatives to the Diet of Mainz that he would adhere to Diether's appeal.[38] At this Diet, Diether personally complained of the injustice of the Curia, in the matter of the Pallium and the Excommunication, and stated that his appeal was not merely a personal matter, but also for the protection of his subjects, and of national interest, and that the princes by adhering to it, would declare to the Apostolic See that they would no longer endure its unjust rule.[39]

The Pope, however, had already written to Albrecht of Brandenburg, on April 1, requesting him to advise Diether to show due obedience to the Holy See, and to fulfill his obligations, in order that his excommunication might be absolved. The Papal Legates also assured Albrecht that the Pope would be lenient to Diether in the matter of the Annates. So, forced both by the Legates and by the representatives of Albrecht at the Diet, Diether promised that he would obey the Pope.[40] After waiting until August, Diether was deposed from his archbishopric, and on January 8, 1462, Pius II published a Bull, requiring Diether, within eighteen days, to give up all lands belonging to the archbishopric,

---

[38] Fontes Rerum Austriacarum, vol. xliv, part 2, Nos. 71, 75.

[39] A. Bachmann, Deutsche Geschichte im Zeitalter Friedrichs III und Max. I, vol. i, pp. 58, 59.

[40] Fontes Rerum Austriac., vol. xliv, part 2, No. 60; Verein für Nassauische Altertumskunde, Annalen, vol. xii, No. 125, p. 184.

otherwise he and his adherents were to receive sentence of Greater Excommunication, and all places where they might sojourn were to be laid under the interdict. The Pope also sent urgent Briefs to Frankfort and Cologne, requiring them not to aid Diether.[41] The Pope also wrote to the city of Basel, and to the Count Palatine Frederick desiring them not to aid Diether. When the Count Palatine adhered to Diether, the Pope released the cities of Lower Alsace from their allegiance to him as Landvogt.[42] The Bull of Excommunication and Interdict was properly published at Strasburg, but in Speier it was torn from the cathedral door. The Count Palatine forbade its publication in his camp, on pain of death, and sent an answer to the Pope, who, in his turn, replied with vigor that the apostolic anathema was a lightning of God that no weapons could withstand. Diether appealed from the Greater Excommunication. His opponents, instead of avoiding him " as a sick cow and a dangerous beast," met with him, at those times when the Bishops' War was interrupted by peace negotiations. Sigismund of the Tyrol, who, as we have seen, was at this time excommunicate, declared his adherence to the appeals. The Council and Community of Mainz did likewise, after some indecision. Their jurists advised this, so that the clergy might not feel compelled to observe the interdict. On November 3, 1463, the Council of Frankfort reported that after peace had been arranged at the Diet, the interdict was relaxed, and Vespers was sung again; with which the common folk were pleased. The Interdict at Erfurt was relaxed also, when it recognized Adolf of Nassau as Archbishop. We see, therefore, that the interdict was observed in some places, but only the " poor people " suffered, the princes were not distressed.

Even the preachers of the Holy Scripture were divided in the matter of the censures, calling each other heretics. On one side, obedience to the Pope was demanded; on the other, Emperor and Pope were derided as the source of all the trouble. On one side was Diether considered a selfish agi-

---

[41] Pastor, vol. iii, p. 205 and n. 2; App. No. 54, Eng. Trans.
[42] Annalen, vol. xii, No. 172, p. 205; No. 185, p. 205.

tator; on the other, as a man persecuted by Pope and Emperor, because of his defense of the German Nation. Bishop Reinhard of Worms protested against the censures, but humbly promised the Pope that he would refrain from further disobedience. The University of Heidelberg, in the dominions of the Count Palatine, appealed, together with the Chapter of the Church at Heidelberg, but to the Holy Ghost, not to a future Council. They protested to the Pope that they were still obedient; begged him to remember the time when he had been their Chancellor; stated that if the Count had asked their advice, they would have advised, at least, his neutrality. Their Doctors, all old men, would be beggars, if the Count would take away their incomes, or the Pope their benefices.[43]

An interesting figure of this period and an illustration of the effect of excommunication on one who is neither prince, nor church dignitary, is Gregory Heimburg, a lawyer and statesman. On October 18, 1460, Pius II sent a Brief to Nuremberg, in which he recounted how he had declared excommunicated in 1459 at Mantua, all those who appealed to a future council, with their adherents, and how Heimburg had adhered to the appeal of Sigismund; and requesting the Burgermeister and Council of the city to treat Heimburg as excommunicate, to expel him from the city, and to confiscate his goods. He sent a similar Brief to Würzburg. In a second Brief to Nuremburg, the Pope commanded Heimburg's imprisonment. Heimburg sent this Papal Brief throughout Germany with stinging annotations.[44] Müllner, the Nuremberg chronicler, says that Nuremberg obeyed the Pope's command and dismissed Heimburg, but he seems to have been present at the Diet there in 1461, and, in 1465, the city declared its willingness to receive him. However, after 1461, he ceased to receive his salary from the city. In Würzburg, where Heimburg's property was, he was entirely unmolested.[45]

---

[43] J. Jannsen, Frankforts Reichskorrespondenz, vol. ii, part 1, p. 231; Annalen, vol. xii, No. 187, p. 206; Voigt, vol. iii, pp. 285-287.

[44] Freher (Ed. Struve), vol. ii, p. 124; vol. ii, p. 210; P. Joachimsohn, Gregor Heimburg, p. 194, n. 2.

[45] Joachimsohn, p. 196, n. 2.

In January, 1461, Heimburg published an appeal to a future council, in Latin. An abridged translation into German was made, possibly by Heimburg, and was spread throughout Germany. The Emperor sent a copy to the Pope in order that he might see the " execrable things which were being said, not only by the greater ones, but by those of the basest condition." [46] Nevertheless, during the same January, we find Heimburg active as representative of Duke Sigismund, at the Diet of Eger. Here he obtained from King George of Bohemia an answer favorable to the Duke in his quarrel with Cusa. In February, he seems to have been unmolested in Nuremberg, and on February 22, he entered the service of Archbishop Diether of Mainz as Councillor. From Nuremberg, he went to France on behalf of the Electors to win King Charles VII to the idea of the General Council.[47]

In 1461 the Pope condemned Heimburg publicly as heretic, and the next day, Holy Thursday, placed his name with those of the heretics of all the ages. Rudolph of Rudesheim, the Papal Legate, advised the Council of Mainz to close the gates on Heimburg as excommunicated, and keep him from attending the Diet, in 1462; they answered him that it was none of their business to admit or shut out those who came to the meeting. The Legate also sent to the Archbishop a manifest in which he described Heimburg as a notorious heretic. Shortly afterward, Heimburg resigned as Councillor to the Archbishop, and it was thought that he feared that because of his connection with the appeal to the future council, it might be worse with him.[48] He then returned to the Tyrol, to his old service of Duke Sigismund, whereupon Cardinal Cusa attempted in an anonymous pamphlet sent to the Duke to get him to give Heimburg up. " The Duke trusts himself to the wisdom of Heimburg. This is not wise, for Heimburg is a heretic; publicly condemned, and cursed with other heretics on Holy Thursday. He is a talker who

---

[46] Ibid., pp. 197-205; Freher, vol. ii, pp. 125-128.
[47] Joachimsohn, pp. 209, 212.
[48] Fontes Rerum Austriac., vol. xx, part 2, p. 108; Joachimsohn, pp. 209, 222.

brings men to woe. Now, against the Church, whose head is the Pope, he cannot win." On August 13, 1462, Heimburg answered him.[49] The Pope permitted Heimburg to be present at the negotiations at Venice, being urged to do this by the Doge, although Cusa had opposed it.[50]

After the beginning of the year 1464, the year when, as we have seen, Duke Sigismund was absolved from his excommunication, we hear nothing more of Heimburg at his court: whether the Duke sent Heimburg away to buy peace, or whether he resigned voluntarily, I do not know. In February, Cusa reported to the Emperor "The Heretic George will no more rule over the people who have followed him." [51] Presently, however, we find Heimburg in Würzburg, where he was not shut out from all communication with men. He still had such friends as Morosini the Venetian, and Johann Vitez, the Archbishop of Gran. When the monks of St. Burchard, in Würzburg, desired to change their cloister into a Ritterstift, Heimburg wrote the petition to the Pope for them, and on December 22, in Coburg, he wrote an appeal to the Emperor for the Bishop of Würzburg, against the Bishop of Bamberg. Cardinal Carvajal wrote him, a few days later, in the hope of winning him back to the Church.[52]

In June, 1466, Heimburg was introduced by the Saxon Dukes to King George of Bohemia at Prag, and assisted him in his quarrels with the Pope. His presence at Meissen had been reported by Rudolf, Bishop of Lavant, the Papal Legate, to the Pope. He sought to gain the Doge to intervene for King George of Bohemia, as he had done for Sigismund.[53] The town council of Breslau reported that " a certain Doctor of sedition and pestilence has joined the sower of heresy (George of Bohemia) at Prag." In February, 1467, at the Diet of Linz, the Veronese friar, Gabriel Rongoni, in his

---

[49] Ibid., p. 225; Freher (Ed. Struve), vol. ii, pp. 255-265.
[50] Joachimsohn, p. 243.
[51] Ibid., p. 247.
[52] Ibid., pp. 243, 250, 255; Fontes Rerum Austriac., vol. xliv, p. 495, n. 1.
[53] Joachimsohn, pp. 257, 275; Fontes Rerum Austriac., vol. xx, part 2, pp. 407-409.

explanation of the Bohemian troubles to the Emperor and
the princes, uttered embittered invectives against Heimburg.
Heimburg's name was among those of heretics anathematized
by the Pope on Holy Thursday, 1467 and 1468. In the
Cathedral Church at Würzburg a friar preached against
Heimburg, saying that he had said that the Church is a
harlot. Heimburg defended himself against this charge in
a letter to the citizens of Würzburg. In 1469, he lost the
friendship of Johann Vitez, the Archbishop of Gran. Bishop
Rudolf of Würzburg at last allowed the mandates of the
Pope and his disgust at the Bohemian heresy, to overbear
his liking for Heimburg, and he confiscated Heimburg's
property at Würzburg, and imprisoned his son Jacob, who
gained his freedom through the favor of the Saxon Dukes.[54]
Several persons opposed Heimburg in the Cathedral Chapter,
among them the Councillor of the Bishop, Kilian von Bibra.

King George of Bohemia died March 22, 1471, and Heimburg found that he had lost his only support. The Papal
Excommunication separated him from the Catholic Bohemians. On August 9 he arrived in Dresden with Duke Albrecht. At his entrance, all Divine Worship ceased, and the
Duke took him secretly to the castle. The Saxon Dukes
sent a petition for him to Rome, asking for absolution, saying that he had never worked in Bohemia to dishonor the
ecclesiastical laws, but rather to the peaceful ending of the
war and to the reconciliation of King George to the Church.
The Papal Legates, Laurentius of Ferrara, and Francis Piccolomini, joined in the petitions. On December 15, Pope Sixtus IV granted to the Bishop of Meissen the power to absolve
Heimburg, and on March 19, 1472, the Bishop freed him
from his excommunication in the presence of the Dukes Albrecht and Ernst in Dresden.[55]

In Austria occurred an interesting case where an attempt
was made to interfere with secular taxation by means of

---

[54] Joachimsohn, pp. 262, 277, 280, 281; Scriptores Rerum Silesiacarum, vol. ix, pp. 177, 222.

[55] Joachimsohn, pp. 285-287; Codex diplomaticus, Saxoniae regiae,
vol. ii, part 3, p. 211.

ecclesiastical censure. In March, 1474, Cardinal Marco Barbo issued a Brief from Augsburg to Ulrich von Graveneck, Heinrich von Lichtenstein, Wolfgang von Schaumburg, and Jorg von Pottendorf, certain Austrian barons, in rebellion against Emperor Frederick III. One of them, Von Pottendorf, had been relieved by the Emperor of the office of cup-bearer (Schenckhambt) and the lands of Von Graveneck had been seized. The Brief bade them to remove certain grievous taxes and tolls on land and water, laid by them without superior authority, and contrary to the customs of the land. These taxes and tolls gave rise to many complaints which had come to him from the common people and the priests. They failed to remove the tolls, but sent the Cardinal an appeal, " such " he said, " that we could not receive it." In May the Cardinal issued a Bull of Excommunication against these four men by name, and their friends. This Brief was issued to all the clergy in the cities and dioceses of Prag, Salzburg, and Olmütz, and " in all other places to which we are sent as legate." He set a new period of fifteen days, and if at the end of this time the taxes were not repealed, the Excommunication was to be declared in all the churches, in the usual form, every Sunday and holiday, candles were to be lighted, quenched, and thrown to the ground, and bells were to be rung. An ambulatory interdict was also to be declared. Divine worship was to be discontinued at any place where they might be and until three days after departure. No sacrament was to be permitted except baptism and the administration of Communion to the sick. Indulgence was also to be allowed. Christian burial was not to be permitted.[56]

The " puntherrn" did not repeal their taxes, nor did they appear before the Legate, nor send representatives, but appealed from the Legate to the Pope. The Legate declared them all excommunicate; and the Pope, Sixtus IV, in 1476, confirmed the excommunication in order that, as he informs us, they might not interpret his silence as agreement with

---

[56] J. Chmel, Materialen zur österreichischen Geschichte, vol. ii, pp. 315 ff., 326, 327, 333; Bachmann, vol. ii, p. 543.

3

their appeal. They were again commanded, in January, 1477, because of the Papal confirmation, within fifteen days to repeal the taxes; "if they do not do this then the Papal See will use against them spiritual powers, and otherwise act toward them as toward the cursed." In fact, the excommunication was proclaimed in the Churches of Freistadt, and in other towns north of the river Ems on the Sunday before Candlemas.[57]

In the meanwhile, on February 2, 1475, Frederick had offered peace to Von Graveneck, Heinrich von Liechtenstein, Jorg von Pottendorf, and the others, and "an Mitich nach sand Erhartstag," an agreement, was arranged between the Emperor and Von Graveneck. In November, 1476, the King of Hungary stated that "the barons whom he (the Emperor) calls his disobedient subjects," had been included in the Peace of Breslau, December, 1474; and that he does not see how he can desert them honorably, therefore, he does not want to disturb them "who are allied to him" during the truce which was to last until Pentecost, 1477. The Emperor had already sent out a proclamation against Von Graveneck and his friends. Then the King of Hungary commanded several Captains, Johann Zeleny of Schönau, Wilhelm von Tettau; and others sent their challenges to the Emperor, as friends of the Barons.[58]

The Emperor, on March 2, 1477, offered peace to Ulrich von Graveneck, and his son Wolff, Jorg and Friedrich von Pottendorf, and Heinrich and Jorg von Puchheim; and among other things, he promised "to obtain from Our Holy Father, the Pope, that they are completely absolved; also to work diligently with His Holiness, in order that the clergy who are excommunicated and *irregulares* will be restored. Also, all priests who because of obedience to the Pope have been forced from their churches, will be allowed to return again." The peace was accepted and the foregoing terms, with this interesting addition—that the Emperor should

---

[57] Chmel, Materialen, vol. ii, pp. 335-338.
[58] Ibid., vol. ii, p. 326 ff.; Monumenta Habsburgica, vol. i, part 2, p. 90; Bachmann, vol. ii, p. 590.

" diligently urge His Holiness, that on the side of the clergy as on our side, the war should cease." [59]   However, the next month, Heinrich von Liechtenstein, Ulrich von Graveneck and Jorg von Pottendorf complained to the Bishop of Passau that at St. Stephen's Church, in Vienna, a command had been nailed on the church door in Latin and German, that they, mentioned by name, should within three days, on pain of Papal Ban already issued, repeal certain taxes or appear before the Legate within fifteen days, in Augsburg, or wherever he might be.   That this same had been read publicly from the chancel also.   They asked the Bishop to remove so unjust a commination, and to see that the process go no further; if he did not do so, " and we come to further shame, then we will seize your property, and the property of all the clergy in your diocese." [60]

While preparing for his Crusade, Pius II in 1460 published a Brief calling for the payment, from Bologna, of thirtieths from the laity, and tenths from the clergy, for three years, on penalty of excommunication. The Brief was read from St. Petronio, the beginning of Lent. " Therefore, many men, not willing to pay, neither confessed nor communed." However, a collection of money was made for the crusade in Bologna.   In 1464, also, Pius II issued an order to the Bishop of Ventimiglia, Papal Governor of Perugia, that, in case the city would not, by the middle of May, pay 15,000 ducats of gold toward the Crusade, he should declare each citizen excommuincate and lay an interdict.[61]   It would be interesting to know if the money was paid.

Pius II excommunicated Sigismondo Malatesta, Lord of Rimini, December 25, 1460.   Whoever associated with him was also excommunicated.   Priests who should conduct worship in his presence would lose all their rights, and his subjects and vassals were relieved of their oaths.   Whatever

---

[59] Chmel, Materialen, vol. ii, pp. 339-341; Monumenta Habsburgica, part 1, vol. ii, pp. 270-273.

[60] Chmel, Materialen, vol. ii, p. 341.

[61] L. Muratori, Rerum Italicarum scriptores, Chronica di Bologna, vol. xviii, pp. 732-733; ibid., Annales Bononienses of Brother Jerome de Burselli, vol. xxiii, p. 892; Pius II, in Opera (1551), p. 865.

princes or communes should aid him were also to be excommunicated. The Pope also wrote to Venice urging that city to have nothing to do with Sigismondo, as he was under the curse of the Church, and they were good Catholics.[62] Sigismondo, himself, sneered at this, asking whether an excommunicated man could enjoy his wine and his food. Venice remonstrated with the Bishop of Treviso for publishing the excommunication, and also bought from Sigismondo, Monte Marciano. Venice decided in October, 1462, to intercede with the Pope for Sigismondo, and also secretly to help him with two thousand ducats. Sigismondo was also aided by Piccinino with money and troops. The French Ambassadors also wished to include him in the truce with Naples. During the Papal siege of Fano, Malatesta was helped by two Venetian galleys. When the Legate protested, the act of the commander of the galleys was disallowed, and the promise was made that in the future he would be ordered to keep his distance; but the help secretly continued.[63] In January, 1461, the Pope thought Sigismondo's subjects were weary of the censures. An image of Sigismondo was burned in front of St. Peter's, bearing the words: " I am Sigismondo, son of Pandolpho, enemy of God and man, and condemned to the flames by the Sacred College." The inhabitants of Fano, one of Sigismondo's cities, besieged by the Papal troops, forced the surrender of the city, September, 1462, through fear of the Papal Briefs. In November, Venice sent Bernardo Giustiniani to the Pope, to plead for Sigismondo, and the Florentine and Milanese ambassadors also united to plead the cause of Malatesta. Among the conditions of peace was the requirement that Sigismondo's representative should, on a feast day at St. Peter's, recant all his heresies; Sigismondo himself should do the same in Rimini. Then he would be freed of the excommunication.[64]

---

[62] Pastor, Ungedruckte Akten zur Geschichte der Päpste, vol. i, p. 132; Voigt, vol. iii, p. 156; Raynaldus, anno 1460; anno 1461, No. 10.

[63] Voigt, vol. iii, p. 123, 167, 170-172; Raynaldus anno 1461, No. 10; Pastor, Ungedruckte Akten, vol. i, p. 174.

[64] Voigt, vol. iii, p. 173; Pastor, Ungedruckte Akten, vol. i, pp. 134, 171, 224; E. Hutton, Sigismondo Pandolfo Malatesta: Lord of Rimini, p. 271; Raynaldus, anno 1461, No. 7.

CHAPTER II

Use of Censures in Connection With the Heresy of King George of Bohemia

Fantinus, the Papal Legate, appeared before King George on August 13, 1462, and declared that if the King continued in his error (faithful to the Compacts of Basel) he was fallen, with the entire family, into excommunication. The King is reported to have sprung up "like a lion," but to have allowed the Legate to leave the hall. The King then addressed his nobles, "You, Bohemian Lords, see how the Pope insults us, and none of you take our part!" Afterwards, he declared that for his whole life, he had lived an honorable life. "It was well known how many wicked Popes there had been. That was no Holy See, but the seat of the pestilence. The Unity of all believers formed the Holy See." The following day the King arrested Fantinus, and in justification of this act, to Duke William of Saxony, he said that Fantinus, in violation of his oath as the King's Procurator, which office he had held at the Papal Court, had attacked the Peace and Unity of the Realm and the honor of the King: " offentlich mit Schriften und andern Handlungen wider Uns und die Unsern." At the end of the year, the Pope, at the request of the Emperor suspended the Censures against the King.[1]

On August 6, 1465, the Pope empowered Rudolf, Bishop of Lavant, Papal Legate, to institute process against all who aided King George, especially those who helped him in his wars against the Catholics in Bohemia, and the men of Breslau. Upon receipt of a Papal Brief, the King of Hungary decided to support the Papal Censures with arms, in order to gain the Bohemian throne. King George sent a letter to the Pope, on October 21, in which he expressed the hope that "Your Holiness will not be harshly moved toward

---

[1] Bachmann, vol. i, pp. 240, 241; J. J. Müller, Des heiligen Römischen Reiches Deutscher Nation, Reichstagstheatrum, vol. ii, p. 248; Fontes Rerum Austriac., vol. xx, p. 288.

us "; denied his heresy, prayed that the processes, if they had begun might be stopped, and that a Diet be held to discuss the religious conditions in Bohemia.[2]

This same year, Hynek of Lichtenberg arose against King George, and the States of Moravia declared war against him as a disturber of the peace. His castle, Zornstein, was besieged, and he fled to Rome. The Bishop of Lavant, Papal Legate, forbade all Catholics to continue the siege of Zornstein, and then threatened with interdict all who should besiege Zornstein. The King had written to Pope Paul II that Hynek was not persecuted for his faith, but for his rebellious conduct, and the Pope answered in a letter to the Bohemian States that he was sorry to hear charges against an orthodox man like Hynek. The King, since he had refused obedience to the Church, had no authority, and Hynek, therefore, was no rebel. Zornstein fell, however, before its besiegers in June.[3]

The Papal Legate Rudolf arrived in Breslau, November 9; ten days later he sent out to all authorities, ecclesiastical and lay, of Bohemia, and of the neighboring lands, especially to the Bishop of Meissen, a notice of his powers of August 6, and forbade all persons to continue homage and fealty to the King, on pain of interdict. On December 29 he sent to the city of Pilsen his Bull of Authorization, and ordered it not to obey King George. The authorities of Pilsen had thought to obtain from the King the right to remain neutral in a religious war, but there were a number of citizens who were decidedly for the King. These royalists were quieted forcibly by the Catholics, whereupon the King sent a body of troops into the city. The citizens complained to Duke William of Saxony of the King's cruelty and supported thereafter the Catholic party. They also sent a delegation to King George complaining of their fear of losing Divine Worship if they remained loyal.[4]

---

[2] Bachmann, vol. i, p. 566; Fontes Rerum Austriac., vol. xx, pp. 362-366; SS. Rerum Silesiac., vol. ix, p. 142.

[3] M. Creighton, A History of the Papacy from the Great Schism to the Sack of Rome, vol. iv, pp. 16, 17.

[4] SS. Rerum Silesiac., vol. ix, pp. 143-145; Fontes Rerum Austriac.,

The Legate on January 25, 1466, threatened the town council and magistrates of Striegau with excommunication for renewing their allegiance to King George. The previous month the Legate had also complained to Protas, Bishop of Olmütz, that " heretics are not accused by preachers, are not avoided, are admitted to the Churches, and to the baths. Marriages are contracted with them. The Mass is celebrated in their presence by faithful priests. Christian burial is given them, and public prayers are said for them." [5]

In June the Saxon Dukes sent representatives to the Legate at Breslau, setting forth the dangers of war with King George. They had indeed permitted the publishing of the censures in their lands, but they thought an understanding necessary. They suggested that the matter might be decided by the Universities of Erfurt and Leipzig; otherwise, a great Diet might be held at which the Electors and the other ranks of the Empire, the representatives of the Pope, and the Emperor, might discuss the matter and come to a common decision.[6]

The Abbott of the Cistercian monastery in Dobarling, in Lausitz, as well as representatives of abbots, prelates, nobles, and cities of that province, sent to the Legate a statement of reasons why they could not answer his summons. We do not know what the reasons were, but the legate said that they " appeared legitimate." As a result, in March he suspended the censures against the followers of King George until further notice. At the Diet of Nuremberg, in November, Fantinus, the Papal Legate, forbade Divine Worship in Nuremberg, while the Bohemian representatives were in the city. On August 20, the Legate Rudolf commanded the priest in Glatz to threaten Hans Wölfel von Warnsdorf and Nikel von Gernsdorf, captains of King George, with excommunication if they did not stop preparation of war against Breslau.[7]

---

vol. xx, pp. 375-377, 387; Bachmann, vol. i, p. 572; F. Palacky, vol. iv, part 2, p. 385.

[5] Fontes Rerum Austriac., vol. xx, pp. 372-374, 387.

[6] Bachmann, vol. i, pp. 577, 578.

[7] Ibid., pp. 588, 589; Fontes Rerum Austriac., vol. xx, pp. 388, 410-411.

On December 23, the Pope declared, in Consistory, King George to be a heretic and deprived of all his lands, which neither he nor his heirs could ever possess. He also directed the bishops and archbishops of Bohemia and neighboring countries to publish this sentence and to command all men to cease regarding George as King, and to cease aiding him or having anything to do with him, on pain of interdict and excommunication. If necessary the aid of the secular arm was to be used. The students of the University of Leipzig, urged on by the rector and faculty, took the Cross, in order to fight the " enemy of God." In Breslau, also, and among the Catholic Lords of Bohemia, the news of the judgment, which was learned first in January, 1467, was received with great joy. The excommunication of the King was proclaimed February 27, 1467, in Pilsen, by the provost and the arch-dean.[8]

King George formally appealed at Prag, April 14, for himself and his subjects, to a General Council, to the future Pope, and to every institution and person loving justice. In his presence were the Dean of the Church at Prag; the Abbot of the monastery of Mount Zion, of the Order of the Prae-monstratensians; the guardian of the monastery of St. Am-brose, of the order of Franciscans Observant; the Vicar Gen-erals throughout Germany of the Order of the Holy Sep-ulchre; a provost and three canons of the Church in Prag; and numerous court officials of Bohemia. King George also attempted to form an alliance, sending especially an ambassa-dor to Louis XI of France, and counting also on the King of Poland, the Dukes of Saxony, the Markgrafen of Branden-burg, especially Albrecht; and his allies in the Empire, Dukes Sigismund of Austria, Otto of Bavaria, the Arch-bishop of Mainz, the Bishops of Würzburg and Bamberg, the Markgraf of Baden, the Landgraf of Hesse, and the Counts of Württemberg, Ottigen and Wertheim, together with the King of Denmark. According to his plan, a

---

[8] SS. Rerum Silesiac., vol. ix, pp. 210-215; Cod. dipl. Saxoniae Regiae, part 2, vol. xi, p. 179; Palacky, vol. iv, part 2, p. 421; Fontes Rerum Austriac., vol. xx, p. 434.

General Council was to be called, " in which, especially, the evil designs of the Pope and the Emperor might be defeated and punished." [9]   In spite of the interdict, Ursula, daughter of the Markgraf Albrecht of Brandenburg, was married to Henry, the son of King George, on February 10.   At the Diet of Petrikan in May, Casimir, King of Poland, denied the right of the Pope to depose a King who had been regularly crowned.[10]

Complaint was made that in the year 1467 a number of " secular and regular priests had in the time of interdict celebrated Mass."   It was said of one of these, an Augustinian Hermit, that he preached in the presence of heretics and excommunicated persons, and had stated that it was the Catholic Lords who had caused the excommunications to be decreed, and therefore they were invalid.   Another is reported to have said: " If I should kill a Doctor, I would go to Rome and be absolved."   Another was accused of giving beer to excommunicated persons; still another, a chaplain in the castle of a certain lord, preached in the presence of heretics, claiming authority to do so.   Of those of whom complaints were made, one, as has been said, was an Augustinian Hermit; two were Friars Minor, one of whom celebrated Mass at a place where the parish priest had left; one was a Praemonstratensian; one is merely noted as a " religious."   Altogether, between thirty and thirty-five priests are thus mentioned as having broken the interdict that year.[11]

King George informed the city of Eger, April 22, that he had heard " how the Bishop of Lavant intends to burden you with bans and other such matters."   He sent them a copy of his appeal, and admonished them " not to break their faith and honor."   The men of Eger responded in May that they would remain toward him as their forefathers had done. A few days later the Legate Rudolf suspended the interdict

---

[9] Fontes Rerum Austriac., vol. xx, pp. 454-457; Arch. für Oester. Gesch., vol. xl, p. 333 (Pazout).

[10] Arch. für Oester. Gesch., vol. xl, pp. 334-337, 367.

[11] Fontes Rerum Austriac., vol. xx, pp. 458, 459.

over Eger, as long as they would have nothing to do with the King and would admit the soldiers of the Catholic Lords into the city. If they should refuse to do this, the interdict must go into effect. Erhart Frank wrote from Prag, June 30, to a friend, Caspar Junckher, in Eger, concerning the excommunication and interdict of all persons and places faithful to the King. "If they will ban, that is their business; we have no physician here, who heals that, as he does other wounds. However, not many have died from the ban." In October, Hilarius, Administrator of the Cathedral at Prag, complained from Pilsen to Bishop Henry of Ratisbon that Eger still remained faithful to the King, and "does not hear the censures of the Church." The Legate, on January 2, 1468, again ordered the ecclesiastics in Eger to continue the interdict there, unless the Council and Town should promise, that after the truce then existing they would turn from King George and publish the censures against him. On August 19, 1469, the Legate Rudolf laid an interdict on Eger, if the city should refuse within six days to do homage to King Matthias of Hungary. Finally, the Markgraf Albrecht of Brandenburg intervened, February 16, 1471, with the Legate on behalf of the city of Eger that their interdict be relaxed.[12]

On September 19, 1467, Hilarius, Administrator of the Church at Prag, informed the priest of Budetic, near Rabi, of the interdict laid upon the lands of Lord Wilhelm von Rabi, because of his remaining faithful to King George, and commanded his strict observance. In the district of the Six Cities of Lusatia, the Legate's work of interdict and excommunication was successful. The people of the district moved back and forth from their duty to their King to their duty to the Pope, intending at first to continue at least the payment of taxes, but gradually going over to complete revolt. In Silesia, of course, the men of Breslau had hailed the King's sentence with joy. In Moravia, where the Hussites were deeply rooted, great commotion arose. The towns of

---

[12] Ibid., vol. xx, p. 490; vol. xlii, pp. 411-412, 414, 418 ff., 425, 445, 509.

Olmütz, Brünn, and Znaim, on May 27, informed the Emperor that, because of the process against King George, and his excommunication, and because of his deposition by the Pope, they must continue in obedience to the Pope and conduct themselves as "pious Christians," and discontinue their allegiance to King George. Albert Achilles, too, hesitated to go to the aid of King George, in spite of his alliance, because of the religious feelings of his subjects. He decided to remain "substantially neutralis." However, "in the German lands and cities," as a contemporary historian informs us, "there was anger against the Pope, and also against the people of Breslau, who were the cause, as all men saw it, why the Pope should stir up to strife the Bohemians, who desired to remain in peace, and have uninterrupted discourse with all people." [13]

At the Diet at Nuremberg, in July, the Legate Laurentius of Ferrara, supported by the representatives of the Emperor and all spiritual princes, declared that the Papal sentence against King George, and the resulting interdicts and excommunications, should not be interfered with. The friends of King George, however, also spoke for him, and the Elector Ernst of Saxony ordered read in public meeting, papers in which George was called "King"; upon which the Legate and the spiritual princes left the room. The excommunication of King George and his friends was publicly proclaimed in St. Sebald's Church, May 15; the Pope declared all treaties with King George null and void, whereupon King Casimir of Poland informed the Legate that he had a treaty with George which he would not break. [14]

The Saxon, Bavarian, and Brandenburg ambassadors arrived in Prag in August, to attempt reconciliation between the Pope and King George. They insisted that the censures should be no further opposed, and the appeal ended. [15] On April 20, 1468, the Pope, admitting that in spite of his

---

[13] Bachmann, vol. ii, pp. 80-83; Fontes Rerum Austriac., vol. xx, pp. 485-486; Chmel, Materialen, vol. ii, p. 295; Echenloer, Historia Wratislavensis, in Bachmann, vol. ii, p. 85.

[14] Bachmann, vol. ii, p. 93; Fontes Rerum Austriac., vol. xx, pp. 472-474; vol. xliv, p. 635; SS. Rerum Silesiac., vol. ix, pp. 232, 233.

[15] Bachmann, vol. ii, pp. 95, 107.

decree of December 23, 1466, some "sons of perdition" had
continued to aid King George, again published a decree excommunicating all such, and declaring under interdict all
towns which remained faithful to the King, as well as all
places where excommunicated persons might be living, or
were received for more than three days. He also prescribed
public proclamations of those excommunicated, by name,
with the ceremony of extinguishing candles at Divine Worship.[16]

The King of Hungary, after a narrow escape from cap-
ture, decided to meet King George personally for negotiations. The two kings met, February 28, 1469, at the village
of Anhrow, and went alone together into a poor peasant's
hut. Nothing written was left of that meeting, and we know
nothing that was promised, especially the question of the
censures. On April 7, the two kings again met near Olmütz
to arrange terms of peace. Their greetings were very
friendly, and, as before, they went apart, and no record was
kept of their words. Later, however, the King of Hungary
invited King George to treat directly with the Papal Legates.
This George refused to do, but his sons and a great number
of followers rode into Olmütz to seek a "hearing" of the
Legates. In all the churches of the city, however, worship
ceased, and the next day the Bohemians left the city unheard.
The Hungarian King continued his friendly treatment of
the excommunicated George, so that the Breslau Secretary
tells us that "all the people were in sorrow."[17] King
George proposed a truce until Whitsunday, 1470; in the
meanwhile, all excommunications and interdicts upon his
followers were to be lifted. The Ambassadors of the King
would be allowed to go to the Pope; and the King of Hungary would send a letter to the Pope asking his grace for
King George, who would pledge entire obedience.[18]

Kolowrat, Administrator of the Archbishopric of Prag,
complained to the Legate, that although a rigorous interdict was laid, many of the parish priests were forced out

---

[16] SS. Rerum Silesiac., vol. ix, pp. 265-267.
[17] Bachmann, vol. ii, pp. 206, 207, 221, 223.
[18] Fontes Rerum Austriac., vol. xx, p. 580.

of their churches, and heretics were allowed in. The mob
was seduced, many running to the churches of the heretics.
Priests were killed, and some consented through fear to the
rites of the heretics. The secular priests observed the interdict. The regulars, having relaxation by permission of their
superiors, conducted Divine Worship, irritating the parish
priests against their superiors. Because of the absence of
Divine Worship, preaching, and every rite of the Church was
despised; and Kolowrat himself was ridiculed at the " Court
of the Heretic " by those who said: " He binds and a monk
looses." He advised that the parish priests be permitted to
admit absolved folk and conduct worship. The Legate answered him, January, 1470, acknowledging that he had im-
posed a rigorous interdict on all the lands subject to King
George, and allowing him to relax the interdict whenever,
in his judgment, that were best for the Catholic Faith.[19]
Permission was asked of the Legate Roverella for the Abbot
of the monastery of Tepl to communicate with King George.
The same year, 1470, also, King George sent a letter to an
unnamed Cardinal in Rome, asking him " to advise more
solicitously Our Most Holy Lord, that His Blessedness would
deign to permit and command the censures against us to be
relaxed." [20] King George died, March 22, 1471, and in 1472,
Pope Sixtus IV threatened the adherents of King Ladislas,
his successor, with excommunication.[21]

At the city of Cracow, in 1474, general interdict was observed because of many excommunicated " foreigners," probably Bohemians, in the city. The Papal Legate, Cardinal
Marco Barbo, gave permission to the Town Councillors to
have Mass celebrated in the Town Hall for their official families, at a portable altar, with the doors closed, and the excommunicated persons shut out. The Mass was to be said
in a low voice, and no bells were to be rung. It was provided,
however, that when the city was under interdict because of
the arrival of heretics, no Mass might be said.[22]

---

[19] Ibid., vol. xlii, pp. 489, 490.
[20] Ibid., vol. xx, pp. 627, 628, 639.
[21] Creighton, vol. iv, p. 67.
[22] Monumenta medii aevi historica res gestas Poloniae illustrantia,
vol. v, p. 256 (Cracow, 1876, etc.).

CHAPTER III

EFFECT OF CENSURES ON LORENZO DE MEDICI AND FLORENCE

After the Pazzi Conspiracy in Florence, Pope Sixtus IV issued a Bull excommunicating Lorenzo de Medici, together with the Priori, the Vexillifer, and the Eight of the Balia, of Florence, by name, "and all who aided in the crimes against the Archbishop" of Pisa, Cardinal Rafello Riario, "and other priests, and who continue the imprisonment of the Cardinal"; and laying under interdict "Florence, particularly, and Fiesole, and the region of Pistoia and the cities and dioceses subject to Florence . . . unless within a month Lorenzo and the others be punished according to their crimes." The Bull charged (*a*) that, knowing the censures incurred *ipso facto,* by so doing, they had given aid to Nicollo Vitelli, and "engaged in many conspiracies against the Roman Church with him"; (*b*) that they had aided in "drawing away the city of Perugia from our obedience, and that of the Holy See"; (*c*) by introducing troops they had prevented a castle from "falling into the hands of the Church"; (*d*) they had secretly captured a castle belonging to the Church; (*e*) they had imprisoned pilgrims to Rome; (*f*) committed piracy on the sea opposite the Papal States, and hindered transport of food to Rome for the use of the Curia. These last brought upon them the penalties and censures of the Bull read each year on Holy Thursday. They were accused also, in spite of their knowing the penalties and censures in the Canon Law against those who violate ecclesiastical liberty and the authority of the Apostolic See, of opposing the appointment by the Pope of Francisco Salviati, as Archbishop of Pisa, and of refusing to the Archbishop, after his appointment, the authority of his position. Finally, they had "hung the Archbishop" and imprisoned other clergy, among them Cardinal Raffaelo Riario. The same month the Pope issued a second anathema. In this he forbade the faithful to trade with the Florentines, to observe their treaties with them, or to pay the soldiers who served under the Florentines.[1]

Even after the first Bull was published, however, Cardinal d'Estouteville wrote to Lorenzo to tell him of the Papal grants of tithes in the territory of the Republic. The young Cardinal Riario wrote to the Pope from the cloister of Sancta Annunziata: " I see an interdict laid on Florence . . . for those for whom I expected and desired good things now evil things befall them." [2]   The Bull created a great effect in Florence, which was for the most part devoted to the Popes, and very religious; and when a herald from the Duke of Calabria brought into the city a Papal Brief of July 7, stating that the Pope desired only the exile of Lorenzo, Lorenzo was forced to call an assembly of the citizens in the palace. He addressed them, and told them that he was ready to make any sacrifice whereby the safety of the city could be purchased, either by his banishment or his death.   But he thought it strange that the Viceregent of Christ should think it right at such a time of anxiety and care to show hatred to a single man by inflicting ruinous war on a peaceful and flourishing neighbor.   In such a condition he did not know if his gratitude toward heaven for the affection shown him should be greater, or sorrow for the various threatening ills which without his fault, had already befallen them.   The assembly declared itself of one accord with him and the whole city took his cause as their own.[3]

The Signiory wrote to the Pope, " Do you not love the people, which you chastise with so great censures? " They then asked him whether they would be free, if they should exile Lorenzo at his command.   His " letters speak opposites; while they promise liberty, they bring tyranny." They prayed the Pope to " give place to those affections which adorn . . . Pontifical Holiness."   They placed themselves

---

[1] A. Fabronius, Laurentii Medicis Magnifici vita, vol. ii, p. 121 ff.; Raynaldus, vol. x, Anno 1478, No. 12.

[2] A. von Reumont, Lorenzo de Medici, vol. i, p. 343; Fabronius, vol. ii, p. 159.

[3] L. Pignotti, The History of Tuscany, vol. iii, pp. 192, 193; Reumont, Lorenzo de Medici, vol. i, pp. 362-363.

with the other citizens excommunicated, "and with the one voice of all . . . appeal." "The contents" of the Bull of excommunication "move" them "all who hear it, to laughter." The keys are not given for such uses. We fear in our times will be fulfilled the saying of the Gospel: 'We will entirely destroy those wicked men, and will give their vineyard to others' . . . We will fight for our religion and our liberty, with Christ our Redeemer and Savior, who will protect our just cause and will not desert his worshippers who hope in Him." To their allies, together with "Louis, the Most Christian King of the French," they also looked for aid.[4]

Bartholommeo Scala, the Chancellor of the Republic, issued, in August, a formal Excusatio Florentinorum. He emphasized the fact that while the Turk threatened the very "destruction of Rome and the Name of Christian, Sixtus, the Roman Pontiff and his illustrious counsellors . . . attack all good men with curses and interdict most bitterly the holy things." He inquired: "What cause is pretended why we are interdicted from sacred things, and separated from the communion of the faithful?" He went on to point out that Lorenzo, from reverence for the Holy Church, had preserved unharmed the Cardinal Riario, and continued: "Thus . . . without deserving it, we are condemned. Because the Pope did not succeed with a filthy plot, he tries ecclesiastical censures." He then takes up the attack on the Archbishop of Pisa: "How justly, how in the spirit of religion, of the Pontiffs themselves, it was done, has been declared in the testimony of the most learned teachers of the law, and in their public writings, because we defended our Palace, our State, and our liberty, which is dearer than life . . . Good God, when wilt Thou pity Thy toiling flock and strengthen Thy people?" He appealed to the Emperor, Frederick III, to Louis XI, King of France, "that you may use your strength as needed, and succor dying Christianity . . . and with Christ, Our Best and Greatest Redeemer

---

[4] Pignotti, vol. iii, pp. 407, 408, 410.

and Savior, who will not desert His cause, consult in common." [5]

The Florentines consulted with a number of canonists with regard to the interdict, and we are told that " Bartolomeo Sozino, Francesco Aretino, Lancelloto Decio, Bulgarinus, Andrea Panormita, Father Filippo Cornio, and other great canonists and theologians " told them " how, in spite of the censures of the Pope, if they would appeal to the future Council, they could have the divine offices celebrated in their city." [6] Apparently, a synod of the clergy of Florence was held, July 23, 1478, at which a most surprising answer was made to the Pope's interdict. Taking up the Pope's charge of the hanging of the Archbishop of Pisa, they said: " O, Shame! an Archbishop, who was never a Christian . . ." Continuing, they said:

> The Pope excommunicates Lorenzo, that most holy citizen, because he does not allow himself to be killed. . . . Excommunicated excommunication! Cursed cursing by a most damned judge, whose mouth is full of cursing and bitterness and deceit! He lays the city under interdict, because he has killed its liberty, as a reward for saving a Cardinal. . . . He slays with briefs, those whom he could not slay with iron. . . . We have found no cause for this his insolent hate and unexpected retribution upon the family of the Medici unless . . . on account of this his Count Girolamo, in whose hands is now the Church of God . . . he raves and rages. . . . Let Sixtus say that he has justly published the censures, but what is the proof?

The censures follow a conspiracy. " Who does not now see that the mad old man wished with these his published censures to wash the mud from the dung pile? " Others will note this. " What believer will not study to provide for his safety through our danger? " The keys are to be used " for God's cause." The Pope adds " censures to dishonor. It is not enough that he has prostituted the Seat of the Pontiffs. He calls Lorenzo, the son of iniquity, who is himself full of wickedness . . . He declare him excommunicated, in order that all good men may know that he is outside of the communion of evil-doers. ' I have hated the Church of the

---

[5] W. Roscoe, The Life of Lorenzo de Medici, App. 15, p. 441 ff.
[6] S. Ammirato, Istorie Fiorentine, vol. viii, part 24, pp. 119, 120.

wicked and I will not sit with the impious.' He curses in order that the Lord may add, above his curse, a blessing."

They also objected that sentence of excommunication was laid without a summons, upon mere suspicion—that the Pope's "wrath, not reason, published this sentence." Taking up some charges of misdeeds of Lorenzo that had occurred long before, they asked, " If Lorenzo sinned then, why was he not excommunicated then? " With regard to the charge of robbing pilgrims to Rome, they answered, " if any merchant was robbed in Florence, he might summon those who transgress before the Papal Judge." They thought that excommunication and interdict were too great a punishment for such an offense, so uncertain, and after so great an interval. They demanded proof of Florentine piracy. " Would that they had never been the spoil of pirates! . . . If they did use a man of this sort to defend their triremes, and he did some crime on his own account, should the innocent be punished for the guilty? Should not so cruel a sentence require some other cause? " They also considered the charge of hanging the Archbishop of Pisa, pointing out that this happened " while the people raged upon the conspirators against their native land, of whom he was the head; while the chief citizens were in confusion at the enormity of the crime. Archbishops do not do such things." They pointed out that he was armed with shield and helmet, that he had forcibly entered the Senate-chamber: " Who would have recognized him as an archbishop and treated him as a priest?"

As to the attacks on the clergy in general, they asked: " Why if they who lay violent hands on the clergy are excommunicated, why are not the clergy, themselves, excommunicated, who lay violent hands on others? Why is poor Lorenzo attacked thus, while he is wounded and filled with sorrows for the death of his brother, and anxious for his life, and for the safety of his native land? Why is affliction added to the afflicted, and a wound added to heal a wound? " They go on to compare Lorenzo and the Archbishop of Pisa. " The innocent man, who was almost killed, is cursed; the murderer and traitor to his country is called a son of

blessed memory. . . . Shall we think, because of censures,
that the blessed are cursed? . . . A curse vainly published,
comes back upon him who sent it." They recall the fact
that the Pope had mentioned sending a Legate to Florence
to offer consolation to the city. "When has arisen a sentence so opposite? So suddenly, pity has changed into
cruelty." As a reward for sending back the Cardinal safe
to Rome, the Pope "lays an interdict on the city." Taking
up the charge: "On account of priests killed," they recount
the crimes of these same priests and affirm, "The ecclesiastical dignity is not permitted in order that the priest may
go about rioting in the Church." The Pope thinks "that he
is the judge, who in his sentence describes only part of the
thing done, and that far otherwise than it was. . . . Who
will fear this censure? Who would not cry to heaven? Who
would not trample upon every religious rite, every kind of
curse, much more this sentence which comes from so vile a
conspiracy?"

They then refer to "the other Sixtus," who "instituted
censures otherwise than this of ours uses them, writing to
the Spanish bishops: 'No Pope should presume to judge
uncertain matters and although they be true, they are nevertheless not to be believed, unless they can be proven with
sure proofs, which have standing in a court of law.' This
one, more Christian than Christ, more Sistine than Sixtus,
proclaims censures contrary to every lawful proceeding. . . .
It is no sentence which has no cause for judgment. The
judgment is false that is based on a lie." They call for a
summons, to some place other than Rome, "in the jaws of
his enemies," in order that Lorenzo may be justly tried, and
if it be just, excommunicated. "The Shepherd of our souls,
as a remedy for a disturbed peace, an attempted tyranny,
an invaded Palace, an afflicted city, Lorenzo wounded, Giul-
iano killed in the Church by a conspiracy, excommunicates
and lays an interdict! O Shepherd, forsaking the flock!"
They appeal then to the Emperor Frederick III, to Louis
XI, King of France. They "implore all Christian princes
and peoples, that when now they see a Pope, elected simon-

iacally, using temples, Cardinals, Masses, to kill the faithful, they may no longer defer the Council." They close with this prayer: "Lord, our God, Whose Hand is over all who seek Him in goodness, keep our hearts and minds, and free us from false shepherds, who come in sheep's clothing, but within they are ravening wolves." [7]

Lorenzo wrote to Louis XI of France, June 19, informing him of the "most wicked excommunication." He continued:

> For I am conscious, God is my witness, that I have committed nothing against the Pope, except that I live, because I have not allowed myself to be killed . . . this is my sin. . . . I believe that God will permit, that He would wish, the one who was defended in the midst of His altars and before the Sacrament of His Body, from these sacrileges, to be defended from this most unjust calumny also. With us is the Canon Law, natural and political right; truth and innocence; God and men. The Pope violates them all at one time.[8]

In the following year, however, Girilamo Morelli, a close friend of Lorenzo, "had the boldness to say" to him that the city was tired; and did not wish to endure interdict and excommunication any longer in order to defend the house of Medici.[9]

The Venetian Senate wrote, July 7, 1478, to their ambassador at Rome, that they considered that the Pope, "at the request of others and to satisfy their dishonest demands," offended against the Florentines, "in both spiritual and temporal matters." He was to inform the Pope, "that we, together with them, and with the State of Milan, most unitedly will defend the honor and dignity of our allies in temporal and spiritual things." The Pope was to be "assured that if he does not recall the censures . . . we will recall our ambassadors and quickly see that we have spoken truth concerning our will." Philippe de Commines was sent at this time as ambassador from the King of France to Savoy, Milan, and Florence, and he arrived in Florence just

---

[7] Fabronius, vol. ii, pp. 137-139, 141, 145-147, 149, 150, 153-158, 160, 162, 164; cf. Pastor, vol. ii, p. 547, n. 1; Reumont, Lorenzo, vol. i, p. 364; Creighton, vol. iv, p. 92, app. 4, pp. 330-331.

[8] Fabronius, vol. ii, p. 132.

[9] J. Nardi, Istorie della Citta di Firenze, vol. i, p. 18.

as the Florentines had gathered to choose the Ten of War. He proposed to the people to threaten the Pope with renunciation of obedience.[10] It was, in fact, a question among the confederated Powers, Florence, Milan, and Venice, whether or not to renounce obedience to the Pope. Florence constantly urged this upon her allies. The Venetian Government, however, opposed it, urging that it was necessary to await the coming of the Count de Clermont, the French ambassador. The Venetian Senate thought that he would have express charge from the King to threaten renunciation of obedience, if the Pope did not recall the censures. But when Giovanni Emo, the Venetian ambassador, upon direct order of his Government, ascertained the instructions of the Count de Clermont, it was learned that Louis XI would only threaten the Pope with calling a Council. There was nothing to do but to agree with the King.

The Venetian Senate decided, therefore, that Jacobo dei Mezo, the Venetian ambassador at Rome, should demand of the Pope the revocation of the censures; if the Pope should refuse, or seek to delay the negotiations, he should consult the Cardinal of Pavia. If the French Ambassador should call for a Council, Mezo should support him; likewise, if the French Ambassador should order the prelates of his nation to leave the Roman Curia, he should do the same. If no results could be obtained, he should retire. These resolutions were submitted to the representatives in Venice of the other members of the League, and apparently approved by their Governments.[11] Accordingly, August 1, the two ambassadors of France, Tristan, Count de Clermont, and Gabriel Vives, with the ambassadors of the League gathered in Bracciano, the castle of Napoleon Orsini, and protested against the corrupt condition of the Roman Curia, and threatened the Pope with a Council, to be held in France, if he would not free Florence of the censures.[12]

---

[10] S. Romanin, Storia documentata di Venezia, vol. iv, pp. 390, 391; Kervyn de Lettenhove, Ed., Philippe de Commines, ses lettres et negociations, vol. i, p. 182.

[11] P. M. Perret, vol. ii, pp. 133-135.

[12] F. Gregorovius, Geschichte der Stadt Rom (4 ed.), vol. vii, p. 250.

A special French Embassy arrived in Rome, January, 1479. It carried instructions which specified that if the Pope should wish to discuss "the censures and penalties which have been passed upon the Florentines for the outrage done upon the Church and the Holy See," they were to answer that the King "would not support any outrages done against the Holy Apostolic See, against Our Holy Father, or against the prerogatives, authority, or privileges of the Church"; that the King would see to it that the Florentines would make "reasonable amends" for any wrongs done to the Pope.[13] On February 5, the Pope suggested terms of peace to the mediating French ambassadors, promising that, since "when peace is made, all arms are to be turned against the Turk, His Holiness would confer the blessing of absolution upon each and all of the Florentines." The ambassadors, also, reported to the King that February 15 the Ambassador of the Emperor Frederick III had said "that the Emperor . . . required only that Our Holy Father have pity upon the Florentines and wish to receive them as a good shepherd." The Ambassador of Prince Maximilian agreed to this.[14]

The League, Venice, Milan, and Florence, proposed to the Pope "that Lorenzo and the city of Florence or those who represent it . . . humbly seek absolution according to the accredited form of the Church, through an advocate or in the presence of a Papal Legate sent to Florence; . . . that an annual memorial be observed at the expense of Florence; that they promise to be good and obedient sons to the Church, the Apostolic See," and the Pope, "and never infringe upon the ecclesiastical privileges and liberties."[15] The Pope made counter propositions. "The ambassadors" of the French "themselves see that it is reasonable that" Lorenzo and his supporters "come personally to confess their sins and to receive the penance from the Holy Father, which will be given them for their spiritual good. . . . For sinners come

---

[13] Lenglet du Fresnoy, Ed., Memoires de Philippe de Commines, vol. iii, pp. 170, 172.

[14] Ibid., p. 203.   [15] Ibid., p. 210.

personally to the confessor, and not through an agent, and
humbly subject themselves to the penances enjoined upon
them by him." Therefore, " securely and without any fear,
Lorenzo himself, with two *priori,* and two *vexilliferi,* who
were in office " during the conspiracy, " and also ten of the
people, can come in the name of the people, to His Holiness."

The Pope also stipulated that " if they wish to be absolved " that they should " have built a chapel in the city of
Florence, with sufficient endowment for two priests, so that
Mass may be said in it, daily; and each year a memorial
be held . . . so that satisfaction be made for the souls of the
dead, and it be for a perpetual monument."

VI. All ecclesiastical persons, regular or secular, of whatever
rank, who did not observe the interdict, and submit to the Apostolic briefs, and who conducted divine worship without any absolution of Our Most Holy Lord: shall not conduct divine worship; nor
be permitted by the magistrates of the cities to do so until the
Apostolic See shall decree otherwise. . . .

IX. That the Florentines pay the sum of one hundred thousand
ducats, because of their contempt of the censures and interdict, to
be used by His Holiness against the Turk.[16]

The Ambassadors of the Italian League met with the
French Ambassadors and showed the answers which they
had received from their Governments. They were to demand
from the Pope an immediate suspension of the censures
against Florence, and if the Pope would not do this within
eight days, they were all to leave Rome. Accordingly, the
following day, the President of the French Embassy, and
the Venetian Ambassador both formally presented to the
Pope in Consistory the ultimatum that " if Your Holiness
wishes to make peace . . . it is necessary . . . to suspend the
censures, according to our instructions." They, therefore,
formally prayed the Pope " that you deem it worthy to make
effective peace, and while the treaty of peace is being made
. . . suspend the censures." [17] The French Ambassadors
demanded a secret audience with the Pope, and " prayed him
that it be his good pleasure to suspend the censures for the
honor of our Lord, the King." In this they were supported

---

[16] Ibid., pp. 218-220.   [17] Ibid., pp. 223, 224.

by the Ambassadors of the League. The Pope answered that
he must consult secretly with the Cardinals. This was done,
and later the Ambassadors were called in, and "after many
altercations on one side and the other, Our Holy Father suspended the censures." On April 6, the Pope wrote to Louis
XI, informing him of the suspension of the censures, "that
we may show Your Majesty that you may know our best
mind and disposition to please Your Majesty and to make
peace, with the honor of the Apostolic See." [18]

The Pope made formal answer as to the suspension and
the short period of eight days. "The rule of justice was
confused. Without doubt, it will seem that the criminal is
made the judge: and the judge the criminal. . . . Our very
censures are held as a jest; and the interdict is nowhere
observed, by order of the magistrates. . . . If they feared
the censures, why did they disregard them?" But if they
did not fear them, the suspension "did not seem a thing necessary to be granted," certainly not "to be asked by . . . the
judgment of the sinners." He had, however, suspended the
censures because of his inclination to unite all the forces
against the Turks, because of the "judgment of our brothers,"
the Cardinals; and because of "the persuasion of the Ambassadors of Caesar, and of Duke Maximilian." [19]

Finally the absolution was arranged for "On the 25th day
of November [1480]" the chronicler tells us, "the Ambassadors of Florence arrived in the city, to the number of
twelve: Francisco Soderini, Governor of Volterra; Aloysius
Guicciardini, Antonio Rudolfo, Bonogiovanni, Gianfiliati,
Pietro Minerbetto, knights; Guidantonio Vespucci, lawyer [at
the time of the death of Sixtus IV, he was Florentine Ambassador at Rome], Maxio Albizo, Gino Capponi, Jacopo Lanfredini, Dominico Pandolffini, Giovanni Tornatoni, Antonio
Medici" come "to ask the pardon of the Supreme Pontiff
for those things which they had done against His Blessedness, and the Apostolic See. . . . No one, either of the
households of the Pope or of the Fathers met them. . . . Only

---

[18] Ibid., p. 227; Pastor (4 Ger. ed.), vol. ii, App. Nos. 128, 129.
[19] Lenglet du Fresnoy, vol. iii, p. 245.

those met them who were their friends or kinsmen." Two
days later, they were admitted to a secret consistory, and
Soderini, the head of the embassy said " that the people of
Florence were sorry for the crimes committed against the
Pope and the Roman Church, and now humbly sought pardon
for them. The speech was very learned." The Pope com-
mended him, and then dimissed them to consult the Cardinals
in secret consistory, " since he was not accustomed to decide
an important matter without consulting the Fathers." However, " he bade them be of a quiet and good mind, and to
hope good from the Apostolic See."

On December 3, the Ambasadors were ordered to go to St.
Peter's to await the Pope and the Cardinals. The Pope
sat with his back to the Church, just at the threshold of the
bronze middle door, upon a chair of purple silk. The doors
of the Church were closed. The Cardinals and Prelates surrounded the Pope in a circle, and there was " a very great
crowd of people anxious to see." The Ambassadors came
before the Pope with bowed heads, and first threw themselves to the ground. " They all humbly showed respect
for him, and kissed his feet "; and then falling on their faces
confessed their sins and asked for pardon. Aloysius Guicciardini, " a man now seventy years old and of great authority
among his fellow citizens " made the confession in a voice
" heard by few, because of the confusion of the assembly."
Then was read in a loud voice, the form of confession which
had been written by Philippus Curvenses, an Apostolic No-
tary of the Camera. The Ambassadors then took the oath
at the hands of the Pope, binding " themselves and the
people of Florence to serve in everything." The Pope then
addressed them, enumerating their sins.

He charged them with being the cause of his war against
them. " Would that you had come in the beginning to us,
the father of your souls, it would not have been necessary to
attempt with arms to avenge the enemies of the Church. We
did unwillingly what we did; but for the carrying out of
our Apostleship, it had to be done. Now, my sons, we receive
you into the bosom of our grace . . . we absolve you. Sin

no more, my sons. . . . You have found how strong are the arms of the Church." The Pope, then, according to custom, taking in his hands the small rods which were to be held by the *poenitentiarius,* lightly struck the shoulders of each Ambassador, who bowed his head at each stroke. The Pope, meanwhile, repeated the " Psalm of Penitence, which begins ' Have mercy on me, O God,' while the Cardinals responded with the versicle." The Ambassadors were " then permitted to kiss the Holy Foot, and were blessed by the hand of the Pope." The Pope was then raised upon his chair, and the doors of the Church were opened, and all went in, to the Holy Altar, where Mass was said. The Pope then ordered his household to conduct the Ambassadors to their lodgings.[20]

Florence and Milan sent to Basel, September 1482, to the excommunicated Andreas, Archbishop of Krain, to see what could be made out of his movement. The Ambassador reported to Lorenzo de Medici that the Archbishop was a resolute man, well adapted to harass the Pope. At the same time, Peter von Kettenheim, the Papal Legate, threatened the town council of Basel with censures. They immediately appealed to the Pope. Already, June 15, the Town Council of Basel had written to the Emperor Frederick III, asking him, " if any censures are issued against us, what we may expect of Your Majesty." [21] The Papal Legate then laid an interdict on Basel, whereupon the Council again appealed to the Pope. Leonard Grieb, the Stadtschreiber, was ordered to complain to the Emperor concerning the interdict, a notice of which was placed on the doors of the Cathedral at Besançon. The Council appealed again from the interdict. Angelo, another Legate, united with von Kettenheim in the interdict, paying no attention to the appeal.[22]

During the months of September and October, representatives of the Council went from church to church in Basel to see that worship was continued. After a short discussion, the

---

[20] Jacobus Volaterranus, in Muratori, vol. xxiii, pp. 113-115.

[21] Creighton, vol. iv, p. 108; J. Schlecht, Andrea Zamometic und der Basler Konzilienversuch vom Jahre 1482, Supplement 54, p. 79; Beiträge zur vaterlandischen Geschichte, vol. v, p. 48.

[22] Ibid., pp. 48, 51, 52.

clergy for the most part adhered to the appeal, among them the clergy of St. Alban's, St. Martin's, St. Leonard's, St. Theodore's, the Augustinians, the Dominicans, and the Carthusians. Those who delayed were summoned before the Council and admonished to haste. The Cathedral Chapter, the clergy of St. Peter's, and the University, were especially rebuked. On October 3, however, they fully adhered to the appeal. The Franciscans, however, did not adhere at any time, but they observed the interdict.[23] The Papal Legates, on account of the interdict, did not come to Basel, but remained at Zurich. Dr. Johannes Bez, a student of canon law in the University, obtained, October 31, from assembled representatives from most of the spiritual bodies and of the University, a renewed adherence to the appeal. But there was greater delay than before, and many complaints were made. The next day, the bodies ratified this adherence, only on condition that an agreement be made within a month between the Council and the Legates with regard to the excommunicated Archbishop of Krain.[24]

Representatives of the Council again met, on November 24, with representatives of the spiritual bodies. "They must remain true to their adherence and have no regard for the interdict, and they will be thought true men; otherwise, there is a brave, but somewhat rough body of people in the city of Basel, which could make bad hours for the clergy. The Council has heard that certain clergy have opposed the former appeals." They were answered by Johann von Gegenbach, Canon of St. Peter's, for the clergy: "Out of love for the Council and for the peace of the city, they would not observe the interdict, until the answer of the Pope and Emperor should be had; then they would do otherwise even at the risk of life." Outside the city, the interdict was considered valid by all the enemies of Basel. A priest of Rheinfeld tore down the proclamation of the interdict; he was arrested by Legate Angelo, but escaped. With forty men he awaited the Legate, and only the very earnest threats of the Ambassadors of Basel made him stop attacking the Legate.

---

[23] Ibid., pp. 53, 85.   [24] Ibid., pp. 54, 60, 61.

By December the inhabitants of Basel began to tire of the interdict, and to ask whether they must suffer for the excommunicated Archbishop's safety. On December 21, the Council answered the Papal and Imperial Ambassadors: "The Council of Basel will imprison the Archbishop of Krain, only they must be free from all spiritual censures and interdicts." They put this promise, also, in writing; nevertheless, the interdict continued.[25]

On February, 1483, the Excommunication of Basel was published, in order to force the Council to give up the Archbishop to Rome. "All lands and cities shall be under interdict into which men come from Basel." This excommunication was very popular outside the city, and the men from Basel were thrown from the churches. On the 12th, an embassy from Basel appeared in Rome asking that the excommunication be forbidden by the Pope. The next month, the Pope wrote to the Legate Angelo: "Cease the publication of the Bull until further orders." September 12, 1484, A Bull of Absolution for Basel was issued by the new Pope, Innocent VIII. On September 12, 1484, the Archbishop of Krain hung himself in prison.[26]

Lorenzo de Medici, in a letter to Lanfredini, Florentine Ambassador to Rome, of August 10, 1487, advised the Pope to maintain in every way his rights as to the homage of the King of Naples, but to avoid everything that would lead to an interdict. "An interdict unsupported by arms produces little effect." King Ferdinand I, of Naples, was threatened with excommunication June 30, 1489, by Pope Innocent VIII, for not paying tribute for his kingdom to the Pope, and was given two months' time for payment and reconciliation. In September, the Pope proceeded, in open consistory, to excommunicate all tributaries of the Church who did not pay the tribute. This was meant for King Ferdinand, although he was not mentioned by name. So the Ambassador, in open consistory, appealed to a future council, and asked for judges, to whom he claimed to show that

---

[25] Ibid., pp. 62, 63, 66, 67, 74, 76.
[26] Ibid., pp. 81-83, 93; Creighton, vol. iv, p. 108.

the tribute was not owed. The same month the Pope published a Bull depriving Ferdinand of his kingdom.[27]

Camillo Senciati, the Neapolitan Ambassador in Florence,
on his way to Milan, in May, 1490, told Lorenzo that " if the
Pope . . . did not leave off his threats of citation and excommunication, His Majesty was not minded to endure such
offenses any longer. The King meant to appear in Rome,
with lance in rest, and answer the Pope in such a way as to
make him see his error." Whitsuneve, of the same year, the
Neapolitan Ambassador to Rome, being refused admission
to the Pope's Chapel, threatened to make his way in by
force. During the month of May, also, King Ferdinand
sent letters to Maximilian informing him concerning the life
and habits of the Pope and the whole Curia; " concerning
the life of the sons and daughters of the Pope, and of their
pluralism," and of the Pope's avarice and luxury, and asking that, according to the command of God, he should look
out for the falling Church of God.[28]

---

[27] S. Infessura, Diario della Citta di Roma, pp. 245, 249, 250.

[28] Von Reumont, Lorenzo de Medici, vol. ii, pp. 415, 416; Infessura, p. 256.

CHAPTER IV

EFFECT OF CENSURES IN FRANCE, ENGLAND, AND BURGUNDY

The Archbishop of Sens excommunicated certain persons who had been imprisoned in the town of Provins, near Dijon, for " vauderie." They appealed from his excommunication. He had previously wished to obtain possession of the prisoners, saying that it was a matter of the Church, but the civil authorities refused to turn them over to him. The matter was also brought, by the Procureur du Roi, to the attention of the Parlement of Paris, who sent a mandate to the Archbishop. He then launched a new excommunication against the prisoners, from which they again appealed. Thereupon, September, 3, 1452, the King's officers imprisoned the Archbishop and took him in person to Paris.[1]

During the witchcraft persecution in Arras, 1460, William le Febvre, Martin Cornille, and Hotin Loys fled from the city, and failed to appear to be tried for " vauderie "; consequently all were declared by the Vicars of the Bishop of Arras to be excommunicated. The notice of their excommunication was posted on the pillars of the churches and the gates of the city of Arras. Martin Cornille obtained from Pope Pius II, briefs ordering a commission to investigate the Arras witchcraft cases. He was imprisoned in Burgundy, and taken to the Archbishop of Besancon for trial. Later in the year, the Vicars of the Bishop of Arras found that Cornille had been imprisoned by the Archbishop of Besancon, at the time he had been declared excommunicated, and declared him absolved. In February, 1461, the Archbishop of Besancon freed Cornille and allowed him to return to Arras.[2]

Charles VII adhered to the appeal of Count Sigismund

---

[1] Arch. munic. de la ville de Dijon, Entendits et Information, in Bourquelot, Les Vandois du XVe Siècle, in Bibliothèque de l'Ecole des Chartes, vol. ii, part 3, pp. 92, 93; cf. ibid., pp. 89-93.

[2] J. A. C. Buchon, Collection des Chroniques Nationales françaises, vol. xxxix, pp. 43, 47, 75, 101; Memoirs of Jacques Duclerc, Book iv.

of the Tyrol, of August 13, 1460. In spite of the excommunication of those who aided King George of Bohemia, Louis XI received his Ambassador, April 20, 1467, with many expressions of honor. The Ambassador states that every time the name of King George was spoken, Louis uncovered. The audience was, in the beginning, public, in the presence of the Royal Council. The Ambassador repeated King George's references to the attempt of the Pope to " show that both swords were in his hands, and all Kings and Lords were his subjects, so that the clergy might better complete their rascalities." The Ambassador also mentioned the " secret contract " of the Holy Father, the Pope, with the Emperor, and that " in order to support the frivolous impertinences " of George's rebellious subjects, he had " robbed him of his kingly rights, had absolved his subjects of their oath of allegiance, and had placed the King under ban." " The Councillors desired to have nothing to do with the King, George, thinking that he desired alliance, because of his necessities and difficulties because of the Papal ban." [3]

Louis asked the Bohemian representative if he had full powers to make the alliance, and the Ambassador in his report to King George was of the opinion that if he had had the powers, it would have been arranged. Louis thought, however, that it would be better that the King of Bohemia be not named in the alliance, lest the Pope might have reason to say that Louis, in spite of the Papal mandate, had taken sides with, and made an alliance with, King George. He would, too, be better supported by the clergy and laity of France. He would send an embassy to Rome, in October, to plead for the King of Bohemia, that the Compacts of Basel would be again ratified, and the citation and the whole process changed in favor of King George. He also asked what was the cause of the difference, and on being told that it had to do with the giving of the Cup in the Holy Sacrament, answered that then he too was no Christian as he had communed under both kinds at his coronation. [4]

---

[3] Senckenberg, vol. iv, p. 390; Arch. für Oester. Gesch. vol. xl, pp. 336-337; 360-361 (Pazout).

[4] Ibid., pp. 340, 360, 365, 368, 369 (Pazout).

Réné, Count of Provence, ordered the diocesan revenues of the Bishopric of Frejus to be seized; Pope Sixtus IV then excommunicated the executors of the order, and laid an interdict on the church at Frejus. The people were compelled to go to neighboring parishes for divine worship. The Count wrote to the Pope, November, 1474: "In requiring of our subjects material sacrifice, has not Your Holiness confounded your rights with ours?" The Pope answered that he had only wished to excommunicate the Canons of the Cathedral who had opposed the candidate which the Pope had proposed as Bishop, and not the Count's officers, least of all the Count himself. The Cathedral Chapter held out two years longer, and then accepted the Bishop who was the Pope's choice.[5]

The Cardinal of Pavia wrote to the Pope, July 16, 1478, that he had heard that Louis XI was sending an Ambassador "of high esteem among them," to say "that unless the censures against the Florentines are revoked . . . he will break off obedience and call to a Council, and recall his prelates and lower clergy." Louis himself wrote to the Duchess and young Duke of Milan that the Pope's war against "our beloved kinsman Lorenzo de Medici displeases us" very much. Again he wrote, to the Duke of Ferrara, "I have written to our Holy Father that he should recall the censures." He wrote also to the Pope saying that he would send Ambassadors "to ask and implore that you recall the censures." If Florence or "our most beloved kinsman Lorenzo de Medici" had committed evil against the Pope and the Holy See, he was "prepared to avenge the injuries to the Apostolic See, Our Mother, and to Your Holiness, whom we hold as Our Father."[6] Louis XI wrote to the Sacred College, informing them, similarly, of his embassy and urging them, "with all our heart, that you persuade our Most Holy Lord to recall the censures." He sent a similar letter to Cardinal Domenico della Rovere, "because of your love to us"; one, also,

---

[5] A. Lecoy de la Marche, La Roi Réné, vol. i, pp. 543, 544.

[6] Raynaldus, vol. x, Anno 1478, No. 16; Lettres de Louis XI, vol. vii, pp. 152, 169, 176, 177.

to Count Girolamo Riario. He wrote again, October 1, to
the Duchess of Milan, telling her that he had learned from
the Florentine Ambassador, " that you persevere in league
and faith with the Most Illustrious Signiory of the Venetians, and of the Florentines, and in goodwill to our kinsman Lorenzo de Medici."   January, 1479, he sent his Ambassadors at Rome a second set of instructions, in which
he said that " in case the Supreme Pontiff . . . in the future
presume to attempt to intimidate us, an appeal has been
entered in the Council of Orleans [1478] ; and it would be
appealed from the Supreme Pontiff, ill-advised, to the same
Supreme Pontiff well advised, or to the next future Council
of the Universal Church, from all ecclesiastical censures,
whatsoever." [7]   In the course of a speech of the French Ambassador at Rome, 1479, recounting the glorious past of the
French kings and their close relationship to the Papacy, he
made use of an allegory out of the Book of Revelation, and
applying it to Charlemagne and the Pope said, " And another
angel went forth from the altar, that is, Pope Adrian; as
it is said to have power over fire, because he had authority
to publish the censure of excommunication." [8]

Louis XI permitted the publication in France of the Bull
of Excommunication against Venice of 1483.   Alberto Cattaneo, Papal commissioner, November 17, 1487, declared the
Waldenses of Valcluson, near Embrun, excommunicated,
relapsed heretics, and delivered over to the secular arm.   On
March 8, of the following year, he pronounced the same sentence upon the Waldenses of l'Argentière, Vallouise, and
Freysinnière in the same region, who had all, previously,
been excommunicated by the Archbishop of Embrun, also,
but without effect.   Charles VIII ordered the Governor of
Dauphiné to aid the Papal commissioner.   The Governor
gathered troops at Grenoble.   The Archbishop of Embrun
celebrated Mass, blessed the banners, and pronounced plenary
indulgence upon the Crusaders.[9]   As a result of this Crusade,

---

[7] Lettres de Louis XI, vol. vii, pp. 178, 179, 182; Lenglet du
Fresnoy, vol. iii, pp. 172, 203.

[8] Lenglet du Fresnoy, vol. iii, p. 236.

[9] J. Marx, L'Inquisition en Dauphiné, pp. 160, 161.

the Waldenses of Valcluson were wiped out. The Waldenses of Freysinnière promised to meet the heads of the Crusade. Two syndics of Freysinnière arrived at Embrun, but without precise instructions. This did not satisfy Cattaneo, and Hugues de Palu, the Governor's lieutenant, and they sent them back, accompanied by their envoys, saying, "If the men of Freysinnière will not come, they would go to them with an army." The Commissioner's envoys obtained promises, but only one inhabitant of Freysinnière went to absolve his heresy, the others fortified themselves in the mountains. The Waldenses of Vallouise took refuge in a cave. They refused to answer summons, and a number of the Catholic inhabitants of the valley joined the Crusaders. The Waldenses were finally either killed or made prisoners. The Waldenses of l'Argentière surrendered, and some were executed, while others were reconciled with the Church.[10]

Gregory de la Tour, Ambassador of Maximilian at the Roman Court, on April 8, 1488, attempted to take precedence in a procession, of the Bishop of Lescar, the French Ambassador. The Bishop refused, whereupon Gregory rushed upon him with his horse, seized him by the cloak and thrust him back. A few days later the Pope announced at a solemn Mass, that Gregory was excommunicated for laying violent hands on the Bishop, and should therefore be put out. However, he told Burchard, the master of ceremonies for the Papal court, that for that Mass, he would suspend the excommunication. Gregory, however, left the chapel, but later, on June 1, he attended Mass on the Festival of the Trinity, in the presence of the Pope, and nothing was said or done about it.[11]

Pope Alexander VI, on August 5, 1495, demanded under penalty of excommunication, within nine days after he had received knowledge of the Bull, that Charles VIII of France should cease fighting and remove all his troops from Italy. Otherwise, he should appear in Consistory in Rome, twenty days after, to hear his sentence. He would hear also that he

---

[10] Ibid., pp. 163-166.
[11] J. Burchard, Diarium, vol. i, pp. 302-304, 310.

had incurred the censures declared on Holy Thursday against the invaders of the lands of the Holy Roman Church. This threat was delivered by the Papal Legate, who appeared before Charles at Chieri. The King exclaimed, in reply, that he would demand nothing better than to go to Rome, but that the Pope should not escape him, as when he had just passed.[12] Furthermore, Charles sent a letter to the Pope, in which he acknowledged the complaints that his generals were cutting off the food-supply from Rome. He would send the complaints on to the generals. Doubtless they would do all in their power to please and serve the Pope and the people of Rome, " to whom we are very grateful, because we were well-treated, we and all our forces when we passed through Rome." He then went on to describe his victory over the Venetians and the Milanese. It had been his intention to fight against the Turks for the glory of the faith and of the Holy Church. " We are not pleased at the shedding of blood, certainly much less than those who lighted fires of rejoicing in Rome, thinking we were dead."

He said also that he had heard that the Pope and the Cardinals had sent money and troops to aid King Ferdinand against the French troops which remained in Naples, " which we have not been able to believe of Your Holiness." A more convenient course would have been an appearance of neutrality, keeping the position of judge, " since we have not thought or done anything against Your Holiness. . . . We hope continually to go from good to better for the honor of God and of His Church, and of Your Holiness." But the Pope evidently wishes to be among the King's enemies, because of this threat, since, because of the disturbance " in Our Realm of Naples, we have decided not to go to Our Realm of France." He hopes before the end of the month to be so strong that Venice, Milan and the other powers will not be able to prevent what he had decided to do: " before we have recovered what they have taken from us, and to show to them

---

[12] D. Malipero, Annali Veneti, pp. 383-389; H. F. Delaborde, L'expedition de Charles VIII en Italie, p. 663.

that there will be no houses left, that we do not allow to stand."

And it will be a sorrow to our heart that there be shedding of blood. It would be better that our forces together, would be directed against the Turks and the infidels for the good of the Church and her glory. . . . On our part, we do not doubt that Your Holiness knows how to work toward that end, with less evil than we can. . . . Whatever happens, Your Holiness will find us a most humble and obedient and Christian son of the Church and of Your Holiness, quick to place body and goods at the service of the honor and good of the Church and of the faith and of Christianity. . . . And when the time comes that Your Holiness and Christian princes are ready for the increase of Christianity, we will be found the first to give an example to the others . . . as we have explained through our ambassadors and letters to Your Holiness.

Charles VIII then complained that the Pope had recalled the privileges and benefices of " our dear and faithful friend, the Cardinal of San Pietro ad Vincula. Therefore we pray that you look favorably upon him, for our sakes, and restore him to his benefices and privileges, as you and the Sacred College have promised. . . . We pray the Blessed Son of God to long preserve Your Holy Church." In the treaty between Charles and the Duke of Milan, of October 9, the Duke promised to demand of the Pope to lift the censures against Charles. According to Malipiero, however, November 25, the Pope regretted " that he had laid an interdict on France," as it had been in vain. " The interdict " had not been published in the French court.[13]

In his Bull of Crusade against the Turks, of June 1, 1500, Pope Alexander VI threatened with excommunication, *ipso facto,* any one of the clergy who should refuse to pay the tithe therein laid, or any one, whether clergy or lay, who urged such action. This excommunication could only be absolved by the Pope himself, or one of his successors. In France, however, it was thought to be a special wrong, that the Pope, without the knowledge or consent of the French clergy, should lay a tithe. Many opposed this openly, and appealed from the censures to a future General Council. The

[13] M. Sanuto, La Spedizione di Carlo VIII in Italia, pp. 579-587; Delaborde, L'expedition, p. 670; Malipiero, Annali Veneti, p. 409.

theological faculty of Paris declared, April 1, 1502, that censures were void and not to be feared, if they were pronounced after an appeal had been made from them; and that those who had thus appealed need not on account of them cease celebrating the mass, or performing other ecclesiastical functions.[14]

In 1510 Louis XII agreed with Emperor Maximilian I, among other things, not to seek absolution from any ecclesiastical censures. The Queen, Anne of Brittany, showed great disapprobation of the "schism" of her husband, and the people murmured at the "impiety" of their master. The following year, on April 16, all the adherents of Louis XII were excommunicated by Pope Julius II. This excommunication had little effect. Louis XII and Julius II were in the midst of a war with each other. In 1510, an assembly of representatives of the French dioceses had declared that a prince who was not a vassal of the Pope, when attacked by him might consider all censures null and void. In the same year as the excommunication, the royal privilege was granted for the production, in the market place Aux Halles, in Paris, of a burlesque, in which a court of fools is shown among whom appears Mother Church, who curses and anathematizes every one.[15]

In England a variety of motives served to counteract the Papal censure. A certain Giovanni Ambrosio de Negroni in a suit before King Henry VII in London, 1486, exhibited a Bull of Pope Sixtus IV, excommunicating all those who purchased or exported alum from Piombino. Ambrosio had gathered a band of English sailors and attacked a Spanish ship laden with alum from Piombino, on its voyage to Flanders. He had captured the ship and brought it to England. A Florentine merchant, who apparently owned the alum, had appealed to the King to prohibit the forcible carrying of the cargo into England. Ambrosio claimed that as, be-

---

[14] Burchard, Diarium, pp. 46-53; J. Hergenröther, Conciliengeschichte, vol. viii, pp. 342, 343.
[15] Raynaldus, Anno 1511, No. 50; Lacroix, pp. 493, 514; Pastor (Eng. trans.) vol. vi, pp. 330, 346, 358.

cause of the Bull, the Florentine was excommunicated, he should not be heard. The case finally went against Ambrosio, and the alum was restored to the Florentine, for the reason, among others, that during Henry's reign no Bulls on the subject had been read or published in England.[16]

At times the power of the Church was invoked to support the State. Pope Innocent VIII issued a Bull, March, 1486, admonishing all inhabitants of the Kingdom (England) to "be subjects of King Henry" and forbidding them "to promote new disturbances under penalty of excommunication." An English version of this document was distributed throughout the country. In a second bull, of August, 1487, the Pope gave to the Archbishop of Canterbury the right of absolution. After the Lambert Simnell conspiracy, the following year, Sir Richard Edgecombe, the Royal Commissioner to Ireland, got the Bishop of Meath to publish the Bull of excommunication, with its easy means of absolution, in Christ Church Cathedral at Dublin. In the oath of allegiance to King Henry, taken a few days later by Irish nobility and ecclesiastics, they swore, among other things, to support the censures of the Bull.[17] Henry, in a letter to the Pope, of July 5, 1487, told of one John Swit, a criminal enjoying the immunities of the sanctuary at Westminster, who had said, "And what signify censures of Church or Pontiff? Do you not perceive that interdicts of that sort are of no weight whatever, since you see with your own eyes that those very men who obtained such in their favor are routed, and that the whole anathema has recoiled on their own heads?" The King continued: "On pronouncing these words, he instantly fell dead on the ground, and his face and body became immediately blacker than soot itself, and shortly afterwards the corpse emitted such a stench that no one so ever could approach it. Verily we give thanks to

---

[16] Cal. State Papers, Venice, vol. i, pp. 160, 161.
[17] Rymer, Foedera, vol. xii, pp. 297-299, 324, 325; W. Busch, England under the Tudors, vol. i, p. 30; J. Gairdner, Henry VII, p. 30; R. Bagwell, Ireland under the Tudors, vol. i, p. 107.

Almighty God, who, of His ineffable mercy has exhibited so great a miracle of the Christian faith." [18]

A Bull of Pope Alexander VI was published at St. Paul's Cross, in London, the Sunday before Simon and Jude, 1502, " by virtue of which was denounced as accursed, Sir Edmund de la Pole, Duke of Suffolk; Sir Robert Curzon; and five other persons; and such as aided them against the King." The First Sunday in Lent, 1503, the anathematizing was repeated " solemnly, at Paul's Cross, with bell and candle." [19] The Duke of Suffolk was then in exile in Aix la Chapelle. In February, 1503, an English Embassy met Emperor Maximilian, in order to have him drive out the Duke, according to a treaty made the preceding year. They reported to Henry VII that Maximilian " was contented to make proclamations of banishment in four of the principal cities of the Empire. We asked that Aix be one of them. The King laughed at that desire." He " intended to purchase the pardon and grace of Your Majesty " for the Duke of Suffolk. In reply " we rehearsed the manifold offenses of the said Edmund." Two days later they informed Maximilian that they had heard that he had given grace, aid, comfort, and relief to the rebels; that he had written a letter to the Bishop of Liège in their favor. He replied that he would give no more comfort to the rebels. About this time, also, he sent a message to the Town Councillors at Aix, telling them that the Duke of Suffolk wished to leave the city; that in consideration of the letters of recommendation of the Duke, which he had previously written them, he would assist with his debts to the extent of three thousand florins. On February 16, the English Ambassadors were told that Maximilian would defer the proclamation of banishment in Aix until his Ambassadors arrived in England; and meanwhile that he would admonish Edmund to prepare to depart, and also his creditors that he would soon be going. A sudden departure would be a great dishonor.[20]

---

[18] Cal. State Papers, Venice, vol. i, No. 519.
[19] Fabyan's Chronicle (1559), pp. 533, 534.
[20] Letters and Papers of Richard III and Henry VII (Ed. Gairdner), vol. i, pp. 186, 189, 204-207, 211, 212.

The excommunicated Duke of Suffolk led a checkered career the next few years, but at the beginning of 1506, he was in the hands of Philip, Duke of Burgundy, son of Maximilian. On his voyage to Spain to take charge of the Kingdom of Castile in the name of his wife, Philip was forced to land in England. During this visit, he held negotiations with Henry VII, which Quirini, the Venetian ambassador reported to the Signory, including the surrender of the Duke of Suffolk, with, however, " a public oath from the King of England to forgive him every injury; to restore his property; and to treat him as his loyal kinsman." During the same month Edmund was brought to London and placed in the tower.[21]

Maximilian arrived in Bruges during the month of January, 1488, at the head of a small body of Landsknechten. The city was in a turmoil. The artisans believed that their magistrates were plotting against them, and they suspected, among others, Maximilian to have been the cause of the ruin of their city. The drill of the Landsknechten in the Burg stirred up the burghers, and Maximilian feared for his safety. He ordered the German soldiers to assemble outside the walls, and, accompanied by some knights, rode to the gate to open it for the troops. He found it occupied by the troops of the guilds, who refused to open it. The sleeping city was aroused. The artisans repaired to their guild-halls, and Maximilian was at the mercy of the city. He left his palace, February 2, and was imprisoned in Cranenburg. From his window, he could see the beginning of the reign of terror which was carried on by the artisans against the old magistrates of the city and the courtiers of Maximilian. In March, Pope Innocent VIII threatened with excommunication the **town councillors, burghers, and all the inhabitants of** Bruges, Ghent, and Ypres, of the dioceses of Tournai, Therouane, and the whole country of Flanders, if, within three days after they had received notice, they did not liberate Maximilian from Bruges. The Flemings appealed from this

---

[21] Cal. State Papers, Venice, vol. i, No. 870; Fabyan's Chronicle, p. 535.

threat, and it was not until Maximilian signed the Treaty of May 12, that he was released.   Maximilian undertook by an oath to accord to the Flemings complete amnesty.[22]

The censure was used both in Burgundy and England, in behalf of the ruler; in the case of Henry VII, against all rebels in general and also against certain ones mentioned by name; in favor of Maximilian against the inhabitants of Bruges and the surrounding towns because Maximilian was imprisoned by them.   It had positively no effect in the latter case.   Henry himself had a profound reverence for censures, which was certainly not equaled by all of his subjects.   The Bull excommunicating rebels was read during the pacification of Ireland, after the Lambert Simnell conspiracy, but here it is impossible to be sure that the spiritual weapons were more effective than the temporal.   As to the Duke of Suffolk, while he was anathematized a number of times, it was rather reasons of state than reverence for the excommunication that caused Philip of Burgundy finally to turn him over to Henry.   The use of a Papal Bull of excommunication in a suit in London is interesting, as showing among other things, how the use of censure had degenerated to be used in favor of a Papal monopoly.   The case was decided in favor of the alleged excommunicated man, not on the justice or injustice of the excommunication, but because the Bull had not been published in England.

[22] Molinet, Chroniques, vol. iii, pp. 297-305; H. Pirenne, Histoire de Belgique, vol. iii, pp. 44-48.

CHAPTER V

Use of Censures by Alexander VI and Julius II

Alexander VI sent by his Legate to Virginio Orsini a demand, on penalty of excommunication and of interdict in all his lands and in other places, whither he or his soldiers might go, together with the confiscation of all his goods, not to do anything directly or indirectly against the Realm of the Church; nor to invade, nor to place armed men in the lands of the Church. He was then threatened also by the Ambassador of Venice and of the Duke of Milan, with an attack. "Having put away the fear of God," he refused to receive the letters threatening censure, saying that he intended to fight against Naples, special patrimony of the Pope, to adhere to the King of France, and not to fear the censures and threats. Accordingly, June 1, 1496, the Pope formally issued the excommunication against Virginio and his family, and ordered their goods confiscated. After the fall of Atella, Virginio was imprisoned in Naples by Ferdinand II, who acted on instructions from the Pope. He died there, January 18, 1497.[1]

In the presence of the Pope, at solemn mass, was read, April 8, 1490, the excommunication and anathema of certain unnamed persons who had caused the Papal messengers bearing executional letters to eat these letters. In all the manuscripts of Burchard's Diarium describing the matter, the names are wanting.[2]

In 1494, Alexander VI demanded the return of Ostia, which had been seized by Fabrizio Colonna with the aid of the French, under penalty of excommunication. He also excommunicated the Elector Philip of the Palatinate, because of difference between the Vassal of the Elector, Hans von Trott, and the Abbot Heinrich of Weissenburg. The Elector

---

[1] Raynaldus, vol. xi, Anno 1496, Nos. 16, 17; Sanuto, I Diarii, vol. i, pp. 254-259; F. Gregorovius, Geschichte der Stadt Rom in Mittalter, (Eng. trans.), vol. vii, pp. 409, 411.
[2] Burchard, Diarium, vol. i, p. 404 and note.

sent Johann Reuchlin to Rome in 1498, as his representative
before the Pope, to have himself freed from excommunication.[3] Reuchlin, speaking on behalf of his sovereign, asked
the Pope to use the gentleness which Christ had exercised.
He praised the service of the Elector to the Holy See, and
the peace in which he had heretofore lived with all men.
Now a monk has arisen against him, Abbot Heinrich of
Weissenburg; if you may call by the holy name of monk one
who with great complainings turns the Pope against his own
prince; and has procured that Philip—who has always been
generous and gracious to the monastery, and had even defended the ungrateful Abbot—has been excommunicated by
the Pope, although it was a purely secular matter.

Of course the Pope did not do this; he would not be so
cruel. It was his officials. He is not to blame, but the
monks who have dared to drag their innocent prince to judgment beyond the Alps. If they had not had justice they
should have made complaint in a land where a just Emperor
rules, against a prince who is Reichsvikar and holds first
place among the temporal princes. " The penalty which you
have laid on Philip is much too heavy. I say this, not to
blame you, or to lessen your authority. It is only new praise
of your goodness. You cannot resist pressing supplications,
even if they are spoken by monks and grounded on perjury."
But such a decision would have evil results. The people
would be stirred up against the clergy. If the Pope himself
decide the matter, he knows Philip, his services and the
acquittal which his lack of guilt demands. For he is pious
and gentle; rather would he suffer injustice. He lets himself be attacked by monks, but he considers the source. " Of
you he desires only justice. He begs of you not to follow
the counsel of those who through human weakness desire
rather to stir up strife in the Church than the peace of the
nation." [4] Presumably, the desired absolution was granted.

Alexander VI excommunicated, August, 1501, the families
of the Colonna and Savelli, on several charges of rebellion

---

[3] Creighton, vol. iv, p. 211; L. Geiger, Johann Reuchlin, p. 46.
[4] L. Geiger, Johann Reuchlin, pp. 46 n. 3, 152, 153.

and invasion and disturbance of the lands of the church. He also confiscated their lands. He named, especially, Prospero, Fabrizio, Marcantonio, Camillo, Mutius, Francesco, and Pompeo Colonna; and also Battista, Paul, Jacopo, Antonio, and Sylvio Savelli. As we have seen, Fabrizio Colonna had already been threatened with excommunication by the Pope in 1494. At the time of the excommunication, Prospero and Fabrizio Colonna were in the service of Gonsalvo, the Great Captain of Spain. Instead of suffering any inconvenience from the excommunication, Prospero, after the death of Alexander, two years later, entered Rome with a few horsemen, against, however, the wishes of the Cardinals. He was promised the return of his property by Caesar Borgia, to whom he in turn promised protection.[5] Sylvio Savelli, another of the excommunicated men, lived in exile at the court of Maximilian, but in 1503 he was admitted to the presence of Alexander.[6]

Already in 1465 the excommunication had been used as a weapon of the Pope against his rebellious vassals. Paul II excommunicated Francesco and Deifobo, sons of Everso, Counts of Auguillara, "on account of wilful contempt and rebellion and many other crimes." He appointed Cardinal Nicolo Forteguerri Papal Legate to lead an expedition against them, arming him with the letters of excommunication, which he read in the assembly of the citizens of Viterbo. When the sons of Everso heard of all this, they sent an Ambassador to the Legate, to say that they had heard with great sorrow of the things done and said against them, that they did not deserve this treatment, and that because of their conduct, and that of their ancestors toward the Popes, they deserved blessing rather than cursing and persecution. They then asked the Legate to help them to appease the Pope's wrath. The Legate answered, in a tone to be heard by the huge assembly, that he thought it unworthy to answer men, excommunicated and enemies of the Pope; that he would not

---

[5] Raynaldus, vol. xii, anno 1501, Nos. 18-20; Gregorovius, vol. vii, part 2, p. 480; vol. viii, part 1, pp. 5-8, 30.

[6] Giustiniani, Dispacci, in Creighton, vol. v, p. 25 n. 3; Gregorovius, vol. vii, part 2, pp. 493, 505; vol. viii, part 1, p. 40.

care to be bound by the bands of so dreadful a censure.
Through disobedience and rebellion they had abused the
Pope's good will; he never condemned any one unjustly. His
advice would be to give themselves over to the Pope in order
to obtain mercy. This answer so disturbed the sons of
Everso, "that they did not know what to do." Towns which
they had considered impregnable were easily captured. "They
began to suspect all men." Our chronicler tells us: "Indeed it is a wonderful thing and a judgment of God that,
without any bloodshed in about eleven days, all the towns
of the sons of Everso were in the Legate's power." Francesco was captured, with all his family, and imprisoned in
Rome. The people of Rome, however, condemned the war.[7]

The town of Ventralla, when the Papal troops arrived,
cried out, "Long live the Church," and Deifobo was forced
into the castle. Later, "in doubt as to the fury of the Lord
Pope and Holy Mother Church, leaving all his lands behind,"
he fled to Venice. The Mantuan Ambassador at Rome reported to the Marquise Barbara that Francesco had been
released from prison through the intercession of Stefano
Colonna. Bishop Aravallo, prefect of St. Angelo, wrote a
letter to Francesco, probably about the same time, exhorting
him to patience. Deifobo was still in 1475 among the un-
ruly vassals of the Papacy. He was received, during his
exile, in Florence, and fought in the Venetian armies. His
property was in the care of the Pazzi family.[8]

Alexander VI excommunicated Julius Caesar Varano,
ruler of Camerino. He charged him with the reception of
rebels against the Pope; with the reception of exiles from
the Papal city of Nucerina, together with the destruction of
the citadel there, monasteries, relics, and other sacred things;
and finally, with the murder of his brother Rudolf. Caesar

---

[7] Gaspar Veronensis, Vita Pauli II, in Muratori, vol. iii, pp. 1014-
1018.

[8] Diario Nepesino in Archivio della Societa Romano di storia
patria, vol. vii, pp. 149, 150; A. de Tumulillis, Notabilia Temporum
in Fonti per la storia d'Italia, vol. vii, p. 130; Pastor (4 Ger.
ed.) vol. ii, p. 413 n. 1; Fabronius, vol. ii, pp. 123, 153; Von Reumont, Gesch. der Stadt Rom, vol. iii, part 1, p. 171.

Borgia seized Camerino, July 1502, and put Varano and his two sons into prison.[9]

The King of Portugal wrote to Alexander VI to inform him of a statute recently passed by him, forbidding any one to ride on mules; that he wished this to include ecclesiastics; that he feared that thereby he had incurred the sentence of excommunication; and that he, therefore, humbly asked for pardon. The Pope answered, October 13, 1501, that so long as the statute was annulled, so far as ecclesiastics were concerned, for the sake of ecclesiastical liberty, he would absolve the King.[10]

The provost, dean and chapter of Treves excommunicated the Count of Virnaberga, contrary to the monition of Emperor Maximilian, in order to force him to Rome for trial. The Count appealed to the Emperor not to permit him to be burdened with this censure. The Emperor forbade all tithes, rents and taxes to be paid to the chapter, unless they should appear before the Imperial Court with the Count to have the case tried, and unless they then paid the damage to the Count, assessed by the Court.[11]

Alexander VI threatened, in 1503, to excommunicate Caesar Borgia, if he did not reduce the castle of Bracciano. It was later surrendered. The Archbishop of Manfredonio was sent as Papal Legate to Bologna, 1506, to command the Sixteen Antiani of the city, as well as Giovanni Bentivoglio, to accept the good will of the Pope, Julius II, and to force Bentivoglio, with one of his sons, to go to the Pope to make new arrangements for the government of the city, under penalty of excommunication *latae sententiae,* ecclesiastical interdict and confiscation of goods. Giovanni and the magistrates appealed to a future Council. Julius II, in his Bull of October, said that "the customs of the city were corrupted in a marvelous manner. . . . There was no reverence for ecclesiastical censures."[12] In this same Bull, it was de-

---

[9] Raynaldus, vol. xi, anno 1501, No. 17; Gregorovius, vol. vii, part 2, p. 490; Sugenheim, p. 376.

[10] Corpo diplomatico Portuguez, vol. i, p. 15.

[11] Dumont, Corps universel diplomatique, vol. iv, p. 60.

[12] Creighton, vol. v, p. 45; Sigismondo de Conti, Le storie de suoi

manded of "those who preside in the rule of the city": the sixteen men who are called *antiani;* the *vexillifer* of justice; the Gonfaloniers of the people, and every inhabitant of the city, under penalty of excommunication, *ipso facto,* within nine days after the Bull was published, that they put out of the city all armed men; that their soldiers shall not fight for the present rulers of the city; that they have no more persons in their houses than the number of servants that they had three months ago; not to prepare arms or warlike instruments; that Giovanni Bentivoglio and his sons were to have nothing further to do with the rule of the city; nor to remain in the public palaces, but to appear before the Pope. There was also published, October 10, 1506, a separate Bull of excommunication of Bentivoglio. Copies of this are rare, because most copies were destroyed by Bentivoglio.[13]

The inhabitants of Bologna were frightened by this threat. The priests, especially, left the city, one by one, for fear of the censures, and even the friends of Bentivoglio began openly to say that it was not his business to keep the Pope from a city rightly subject to the Church. Chaumont, the French general, promised that the family of Bentivoglio would be in protection of the King of France, if, within three days he gave up his power to the Church. He could have liberty to reside in Bologna. Bentivoglio and his sons hastened to ask for the arbitration of the French. Chaumont obtained from Julius II for Bentivoglio the right to retire from Bologna, to dwell in the Duchy of Milan and enjoy all the income from his estate. After Giovanni Bentivoglio and his family had left the city, the people of Bologna sent representatives to Julius II surrendering the city and desiring absolution of all censures. Bentivoglio lived under French protection in Milan. Later Louis XII of France took away his protection, and Bentivoglio fled to Venice. Venice refused to give him up to the Pope, pleading the right of asylum.[14]

---

tempi dal 1475 al 1510, vol. ii, p. 350; Raynaldus, vol. xi, anno 1506, Nos. 25-27.

[13] Ibid., Pastor (4 Ger. ed.) vol. iii, p. 613 n. 3.

[14] Sigismondo de Conti, vol. ii, pp. 352, 354; F. Guicciardini, The History of Italy, vol. iv, pp. 35, 36; Creighton, vol. v, p. 113.

Julius II issued a threat, April, 1509, to the Doge, councillors and citizens of Venice, that, if within twenty-four days after the posting of the Bull on the doors of St. Peter's they did not give up the cities of Ravenna and Faenza, the territory of Imola and all other lands and cities which they had seized from the church, with the revenues therefrom, and put any impediment in the way of these cities returning to the obedience of the Church, he would pronounce the sentence of greater excommunication upon them; from which there would be no absolution except by the Roman Pontiff. If they remained obdurate three days beyond the twenty-four, he laid the ecclesiastical interdict on all the cities and lands possessed by the Venetians. If they still remained obdurate three days later, he declared the oath of allegiance of all lands and cities subject to Venice void. The excommunicated persons should not be allowed to give testimony, to make wills, nor to sue in the courts, and their debtors were to be free of their debts. Julius II further required of all courts, Italian, French, German, Spanish, English or Scotch, in which the Venetians should win suits, that they shall hold the property won as long as the interdict should remain in force. All inhabitants of all cities were to have nothing to do with those excommunicated, neither to buy from them, nor to sell to them, nor to send them grain, wine, and other food, arms or ammunition, on penalty of excommunication. Julius admonished, also, all clergy, of whatever rank, six days after the twenty-four, to leave the lands until the interdict is relaxed. If any ecclesiastic refused, he should be, *ipso facto,* excommunicated and deprived of his benefice, except that enough should remain to look after the church property and to baptize infants likely to die. Any monasteries in which mass and other Divine Worship is celebrated should lose all privileges. No cities or princes should aid the Venetians with soldiers or money, on penalty of excommunication. All clergy, everywhere, should, in their Churches, on the Lord's Day and other festivals, publicly announce the excommunication, under the banner of the cross, with the ringing of bells, and candles raised and then thrown to the ground and extinguished, and other customary ceremonies. He also excommunicated those who hindered the sending, posting, or publishing of copies of these letters.[15]   The Bull stated further that the Venetians had already shown their contempt for censures, by allowing the Bentivogli in their territory.

The Council of Ten did not allow any publication of the Bull in Venice, strictly forbade any one to receive it, and deputed guards to watch all the high walls and tear down any notice they might find on them. They also ordered certain Doctors of Canon Law to compose an appeal to a future Council, which they ordered sent to the Patriarch of Constantinople in Hungary, as a very dear friend of the city, and one who could call a Council. They also sent two couriers to post the appeal on the doors of St. Peter's, which greatly angered the Pope. The appeal was also scattered about the streets of Rome, to a future Council, and " in default of human justice, to the tribunal of Christ, the most just Judge, and supreme Lord of all." [16]   On May 4, six hundred copies of the Bull were being printed in Rome, to send to Venice, and to all the world. Julius II told the Orsini that he absolved them from keeping the money of Venice, as excommunicated persons. " Do not return the money." Three thousand ducats, however, were returned. No mass was said in any of the Churches of Venice, even in St. Mark's. Sigismondo de Conti says that in the Battle of Ghiadadda, May 14, 1509, " Reverence for the censures, and the wrath of God, tore the weapons from the hands of the Venetians." After this battle, the people subject to Venice either inclined to rebel, or were averse to suffer for their sake.[17]

The Venetian Cardinals Griniano and Cornaro demanded of Julius, in the name of the Senate, absolution as their due, because they had made restitution of the towns within

---

[15] The Bull, in Sanuto, I Diarii, vol. viii, pp. 187-204.

[16] Romanin, vol. v, p. 202; Guicciardini, vol. iv, p. 235; Sanuto, I Diarii, vol. viii, pp. 161, 162, 310.

[17] Guicciardini, vol. iv, p. 254; Sigismondo de Conti, vol. ii, p. 390; Sanuto, I Diarii, vol. viii, p. 170, 182.

the term of twenty-four days. The Pope answered that they had not yielded obedience, had offered the towns with conditions, and held back the revenues. The Council of Ten also protested as to the terms of absolution. The Pope, ill-informed, refused absolution except on unjust terms. " Affected by so many evils, the Venetians decided to make peace with Pope Julius, that they might flee the wrath of God." They sent letters offering to send as Ambassadors six of the principal senators. It was agreed in Consistory that they should be admitted, but this was opposed by the ambassadors of the Emperor and of the King of France. The Pope, they said, was obligated to prosecute the Venetians with both spiritual and temporal arms. Julius answered that he would not grant the absolution until the Emperor should gain what belonged to him.[18]

The six envoys arrived in Rome in July. They came at night, as excommunicated, and they did not meet the Pope. Their entrance was opposed by the Emperor, Spain, and France, but the Archbishop of York, the English Ambassador, favored it. Julius II answered the objectors that it was not his duty to continue prosecuting with spiritual arms; that the Venetians were repentant, and to withhold the absolution would be a harm to souls. The towns had been restored, and the restitution of revenue was unimportant. He would continue to adhere to the League of Cambrai with temporal arms. However, " the Pope took care of the dignity of the Roman See." He asked that they denounce the appeal; put no tax on ecclesiastics; that they should not hinder the carrying of suits to the Roman Curia; that they would allow the Pope to appoint whom he would to bishoprics and monasteries; that they would give to the subjects of the Roman Church the right of free navigation on the Adriatic; that they would no longer maintain a magistrate at Ferrara. The Ambassadors answered that the tithes had been granted to the city by Pope Paul II for fighting the Turks, and that no state had done more for the Popes than

[18] Creighton, vol. v, p. 117; Guicciardini, vol. iv, pp. 273, 274, 276, 277; Sigismondo de Conti, vol. ii, pp. 400-403.

Venice. Finally, the absolution was pronounced in due form, February 25, 1510.[19]

This was the second excommunication of Venice during our period. On May 24, 1483, Pope Sixtus IV in a public consistory declared the Signoria of Venice excommunicated, if within fifteen days they should not restore to the Duke of Ferrara what they had seized from him. He laid an interdict on Venice, and ordered the religious to leave Venice within three days. On May 25, the Bull was fixed to the door of St. Peter's. When they heard of this, the Signoria ordered the Patriarch of Venice to publish no Bull that might come from Rome, but immediately to give it to them. On June 2, they commanded all watchmen of the city to search diligently at all doors of churches for any writing that might be posted. But the Bull was brought into the city by the road from Mantua, the least expected, and given to the Patriarch. Francesco Diedo, the Venetian Ambassador, had left Rome before the Bull was published, but his representative refused to carry it to Venice. The Patriarch was commanded, under penalty of excommunication and suspension, to communicate the Bull to the Doge and Signoria.

He feigned illness, but secretly informed the Doge and the Council of Ten. They enjoined on him the most rigorous secrecy and ordered him to maintain worship, as heretofore. The same month the Papal Legate published the Bull in Ferrara, and a Carmelite monk preached in the Plaza that the people should be faithful to their own Duke, and not submit to the Signoria of Venice. The Bull was also published in Milan. The Signoria decided to appeal to a future Council, and named a committee of five prelates and students of Canon law to examine the question. These all approved the appeal. A copy of the appeal was carried by messenger to Rome and fixed to the door of the Church of San Celso. On June 15, before the Patriarch of Constantinople, as first President of the future Council, sitting with

---

[19] Guicciardini, vol. iv, p. 312; Sigismondo de Conti, vol. ii, pp. 400-403.

many other prelates, an appeal was made in the name of the Signoria of Venice to the future Council. This the Patriarch received favorably and suspended the sentence of interdict. The Signoria, on July 5, decided that all the income of the Venetian prelates and priests who had not returned from Rome should be retained. The people of Rome tore down the Bulls of excommunication throughout the city, saying that the King of Apulia, who had, the previous year, led his army against the gates of Rome and besieged the city, had not been excommunicated, but that the Signoria, who had freed it, were excommunicated.[20]

In public consistory August 9, 1510, Julius II proposed the excommunication of Alfonso, Duke of Ferrara. He and the House of Este were ordered to give up Ferrara, otherwise all his lands were laid under interdict, and those with him in camp were to be excommunicated without exception. He was charged with making salt at Comaccio at the cost of the Papal mines at Cervia. He was also said to be a rebel, and to have aided Cardinal d'Amboise, who desired the tiara. Some of the Cardinals desired to postpone the matter to another consistory. One Cardinal continued to vote against the excommunication, on the ground that the King of France could not support it, because of his obligation to the Duke of Ferrara, and because of the things done recently against Genoa by the Pope. Julius II, also, he said, "seized territories to give them to his nephews." Julius answered that he was not gaining territory for his nephews, but for the Church. Several other Cardinals voted against the excommunication.

The Bull was ordered published in Bologna, and was also posted in the Church of St. John Lateran. The Duke, attacked by the Papal troops, called his people to his defense, and all responded eagerly. Nobles, doctors of the University, merchants, artisans, aged men, women and children, even the clergy, all assisted in building the fortifications of the city. The Papal Legate at Bologna threatened the French

---

[20] Romanin, vol. iv, pp. 413, 414; Navagiero, Storia della republica Venezia, in Muratori, vol. xxiii, pp. 1182-1184.

General with excommunication unless he ceased aiding the Duke of Ferrara. He answered that he would hang the Legate's messengers if they came back again. The Duke of Ferrara, on October 5, sent to Louis XII of France a manifesto, in which he complained that, previous to the excommunication, Julius II had summoned him to Rome within twelve days. The citation had been posted on the doors of the cathedral at Bologna, and when the twelve days were up, the sentence of excommunication was pronounced. He contested, therefore, the validity of the sentence, because he had not been present to defend himself, and further, if he had gone to Rome he would have put himself into great danger. However, the Pope won in this contest, for on July 4, 1512, after the French army had left Italy, Duke Alfonso, armed with a Papal safe-conduct, prostrated himself before Julius and humbly implored absolution, which was willingly granted.[21]

Julius II excommunicated the French General, Chaumont, October 14, 1510. The General, with all his forces, advanced against Bologna, where Julius then was. When the news reached the city, there was a great uproar, as well among the nobles as the common people. Julius, by many concessions, invited the people of the city to take up arms in his defense, but without effect. Chaumont was later stricken with fever and died February 11, 1511. Before his death, he declared " with great marks of devotion," his sorrow for the offenses he had committed against the Church, and obtained the absolution, which he sought.[22]

Julius II excommunicated all the adherents of King Louis XII of France, on April 16, 1511. On July 18 he declared that all those who adhered to the Edict of May 16, convoking a Council at Pisa, brought upon themselves the severest penalties of the Church, and all cities and districts supporting them were laid under the Interdict. The Bishop of Paris

[21] Sanuto, I Diarii, vol. xi, pp. 108, 112; Pastor, (Eng. trans.), vol. vi, pp. 328, n. 4, 419; Noyes, pp. 176, 179; Lettres de Louis XII, vol. i, p. 282; Creighton, vol. v, p. 129.

[22] Raynaldus, anno 1510, No. 16; Giucciardini, vol. v, pp. 115, 116, 119, 173.

as Ambassador of the King of France, and the representatives of Emperor Maximilian, had agreed with certain Cardinals on this edict. Julius, driven from Rome, could see his citation to the Council nailed to the church doors at Rimini. The King of Spain would have nothing to do with the Council. His Ambassador, May 21, 1512, read publicly a letter to the Pope from His Majesty, saying that he had learned that a conciliabulum had convened in Pisa, to the injury of the Holy Mother Church and against the honor of the Most Holy Pope Julius, " whom I have confessed to be true Pope and rightly elected." He would not support it, and would do everything to destroy such a conciliabulum.[23]

The Emperor tried to gain support for the Council in Poland, and with the King of Hungary, but in vain. The Abbot Trithemius advised him that Germany would not follow its Emperor in this matter. The Bishop of Brixen, because of his obligation to the Pope, refused to be Imperial representative to the Council, and the Archbishop of Salzburg, because of his oath, would not even send one of his councillors. The Emperor's daughter, Marguerite, wrote him September, 1511, that "for the honor and reverence of God" he "ought not to meddle with the assembly of the Council, which would be held at Pisa." He "ought to let it alone and please the Pope, to whom recognition belongs." The intrigues of the schismatic Cardinals, through the month of September, filled the Pope with anxiety. On August 10, however, the Venetian Ambassador reported from Florence that the matter of the Council was "empty and cold." September 20, Cardinal de Prie wrote to King Louis XII of France, that unless he would exert his royal power in favor of the assembly at Pisa, it would be a complete failure. The French Court Bishops followed the King in support of the Council. The Milanese jurist Decius, and the Carthusian Abbot Zaccaria Ferreri also supported the Council. The hermit Angelo of Vallombrosa adjured Cardinal Carvajal not to rend the unity of the Church; what he was doing, he

---

[23] Pastor, (Eng. trans.) vol. vi, pp. 372, 373; H. Ulmann, Kaiser Maximilian I, vol. ii, pp. 434, 435; Sanuto, vol. xiv, p. 243.

said, was like the crime of Lucifer and would bring God's judgment upon him.   Thomas de Vio, of Gaeta, better known as Cajetan, General of the Dominicans, wrote several works against the Council, which were publicly burned by Louis XII.   Florence attempted either to have the Council postponed or held at some other place than Pisa; but the King of France was firm and Florence yielded.[24]

For this Julius II laid an interdict on Florence, against which the city appealed to a Council.   In October, some Frenchmen, the Bishop's officials, arrived at Pisa, and found the popular feeling so much against them that they had to seize their quarters by force.   Florence stated that she would treat the Cardinals as enemies if they came with armed men, and for this, the interdict was suspended for fourteen days.   On October 24, the Cardinals Carvajal, Briconnet, Francesco Borgia, and de Prie were excommunicated by the Pope, and Cardinals San Severino and d'Albret were threatened with like punishment if they continued disobedient.   Soon after this, Cardinal Francesco Borgia died. In the course of their journey to Pisa, the schismatic, and now excommunicated Cardinals encountered much hostility on the part of the populace.   In Prato and Pistoja they found the churches and inns closed; everyone fled from them; and in Pisa itself they could only get lodgings at the command of the Florentine commissioners.[25]

The Council could not commence its meetings on November 1 in the Cathedral, because at the Pope's command the Canons had locked all the doors; but on November 5 the excommunicated Cardinal Carvajal celebrated mass in the Cathedral, assisted by Cardinal Briconnet, also excommunicate.   He then gave the official call to the Council, at which service were present four Cardinals and eighteen bishops and abbots.   The excommunicated Carvajal was proclaimed President of the Council, and Odet de Foix, Guardian.   All the

[24] Ulmann, vol. ii, pp. 433, 434; Pastor, (Eng. trans.) vol. vi, pp. 373-375, 385-389; Sanuto, vol. xii, p. 371; vol. xiii, p. 201.
[25] Pastor, (Eng. trans.) vol. vi, pp. 374, 375, 385-389; Sanuto, vol. xiii, pp. 177, 201; Cerretani's Chronicle, in Pastor, (Eng. trans.) vol. vi, p. 389.

censures of the Pope against the Council were declared null
and void. The Ambassador Francesco came from Florence
to encourage the Cardinals and prelates, and there were also
present representatives of the King of France. Abbot Ferreri made an address calling for the reformation of the
Church. The sentence of excommunication was laid against
all who should speak or write against the Council or interfere
with it! A body presided over by excommunicated men, excommunicating its opponents! The Council also stated that
the Pope had no right to cite to Rome for any cause during
the Council, except as the Council might permit. They decided to leave Pisa because of the war and meet in Milan on
December 15, and also to send ambassadors to the Pope,
"praying His Holiness" to come to the Council and to
select a safe place for it. If the Pope would not choose a
place, they would choose one as second best.[26] While still
in Pisa, a crowd assembled under the windows of the palace
inhabited by Carvajal, where the schismatics were gathered
together, shouting "Kill them." In Milan both people and
clergy kept to themselves. Upon the entrance of the schismatic Cardinals into the city, December 7, no Bishop appeared to greet them. The majority of the clergy observed
the Interdict, in spite of the threats of the French Governor
General, while the populace jeered at the "Anti-Papal Mas-
queraders." [27]

After the death of Julius II, at the conclave held to elect
a new Pope, a letter was received from Cardinal Carvajal,
stating that the former Pope had deprived him of the office
of Cardinal unjustly, and that he desired to appear de jure.
In March, 1513, Cardinals San Severino and Carvajal sailed
from Marseilles, landed in Italy, and were taken to Pisa,
where they were kept under guard. The Emperor wrote to
Leo X in their behalf, as did the Ambassador of the French
King. In June, at a meeting of the Lateran Council, letters were received from " Bernardo Carvajal," and " Frederico
San Severino," recalling and condemning the Council of

---

[26] Sanuto, vol. xiii, p. 233; vol. xiv, pp. 330-332.
[27] Pastor, (Eng. trans.) vol. vi, p. 393.

Pisa, and praising and approving the present one, as legitimate and true and ecumenical, and asking pardon. It was
decided that they should enter into the consistory, should
ask for pardon, and should return in the garb of the Cardinal. The night of June 27 the two Cardinals entered
Rome, and the following morning the master of ceremonies
vested them in purple mantles, and they went before the
Pope in consistory, who rebuked them. Then the Cardinals
were reinstated and went to eat with the Pope. The English
and Swiss Cardinals, Bainbridge, Archbishop of York, and
Matthaeus Schinner, refused to be present at the reinstate-
ment.[28]

Thomas Resch, the Rector of the University of Vienna,
excommunicated the Doctors of Theology of his university.
They appealed to the Pope, July 7, 1513, and also to the
Emperor, held themselves not excommunicated, and continued to attend Divine Worship. Resch had been chosen
Rector, but not being a Doctor of Theology, merely a Bach-
elor, they had not recognized him. When, however, they
found that they had committed an irregularity, they begged
" simpliciter et eventualiter," for absolution from the excommunication of the Pope. He ordered their absolution in a
letter, November 6, 1513, to the provost of the Church of St.
Dorothea, in Vienna.[29]

Leo X threatened Francesco Maria della Rovere, Duke of
Urbino, together with all his adherents, with excommunication, on March 1, 1516, unless within eighteen days he appeared personally before the Pope, because he had aided the
Pope's enemies. Rovere did not appear, but sent the Dow-
ager Duchess, Elizabeth Gonzaga, who was received by the
Pope, who said that the Duke must unreservedly submit. An
interdict was laid on the Duke by Leo X in February, 1517.
In the meanwhile, he had been deprived of his duchy by
the Pope, and had fled with his family to Mantua. Now he
returned, supported secretly by Odet de Foix, French General in Lombardy and with Italian, German, Spanish and

[28] Sanuto, vol. xvi, pp. 58, 72, 308, 400, 432, 433.
[29] Kink, vol. i, part 1, pp. 118, 119.

Gascon mercenaries. As he entered his duchy of Urbino, he was received everywhere with joy by the people. In Rome there was complete surprise. Leo trusted neither France nor Venice, knowing that the Duke must be supported by one or the other. In September the war was ended by the mediation of Spain and France; the Duke was absolved of his censures and was allowed to return to Mantua, abandoning all his duchy.[30]

There was frequent use of the censure during this period. Evidently those ecclesiastics who used it had faith in its effectiveness—indeed, one of them spoke of it as " the lightning of God." It was used for various reasons, most of them so trivial as to lessen its effect. The politics of the Papal States caused it to be used quite often against rebellious nobles, against neighboring states, to drive out despots from cities claimed by the Pope, in punishment for seizing Papal territory. Even in two cases where fratricide and the hanging of an archbishop are charged, the political motive for its use appears so strongly that the charge seems a pretext. It was used also for ecclesiastical reasons as a weapon against heresy; to collect money for a crusade; to enforce closure upon a convent; to enforce the payment of the annates; and to drive a deposed Archbishop from his territory.

The excommunication did not enforce itself. The one who issued it would write letters to cities and princes reminding them of, and urging upon them, their duties arising from it. As to its real effect, it is difficult to determine, as armies would assist the spiritual weapons. In fact, Lorenzo de Medici, who had been excommunicated and absolved himself, advised Pope Innocent VIII that " an interdict unsupported by armies produces little effect." Usually the one excommunicated would appeal to the Pope better informed, to a future Pope, to a future General Council; and even to the Holy Spirit; and to the whole body of believers. This in spite of the fact that an appeal to a future General Council was

---

[30] Pastor (4 Ger. ed.) vol. iv, part 2, pp. 115, 144, and app. 16, p. 684; Von Reumont, Gesch. der Stadt Rom, vol. iii, part 2, pp. 91-93; Guicciardini, vol. vii, part 14, p. 88.

made a reason for excommunication *ipso facto* by Pope Pius II, in 1459. He would also deny that the excommunication really existed, since it was unjust, and he would sneer at it. He would attack the moral life of the ecclesiastic who issued it. He would send dire warnings and threats of coming with an army against him, or of depriving him and his clergy of their churches and livings. In the cases of princes, either of Church or State, the excommunications had little effect; but in the case of a man " of the baser sort," while he might at first hurl defiance, sooner or later, deserted by his friends, with his property confiscated, he would seek absolution.

In Germany the national feeling against the Curia affected the reception of excommunication, and excommunications were listed among the grievances of the German nation against the papacy. An excommunicated Archbishop, having appealed to a future General Council, called on other princes to adhere to his appeal, as he was fighting their fight as well as his own. In France, while each of the kings from Louis XI to Louis XII, personally, had little regard for excommunication, yet in their court and among the nation at large, the old reverence for the censures remained. Toward the end of this period, from about 1500 onward, there was decidedly greater independence of the clergy, however, the theological faculty of Paris declaring, 1502, that censures were void and not to be feared if they were pronounced after an appeal had been made from them.

Another difficult problem presents itself in the relation between heresy and excommunication. The adherents of heretics were excommunicated, and a body of reputed heretics might be excommunicated providing they did not recant. On the other hand, to disregard a censure was heresy. Undoubtedly it was the heresy and not the excommunication that stirred up most opposition. Crusades were organized during this period against heretics. In the well-known case of King George of Bohemia, it is likely, and, in fact, was charged by contemporaries, that his political quarrel with the Catholic nobles, and with the inhabitants of Breslau, was the real cause of the disturbance.

If the excommunication of princes was ineffective, the same thing cannot be said with regard to the interdict. The care with which the governments of cities placed under the interdict guarded against the approach of a messenger carrying the notice of the interdict; the fact that they sought the advice of canonists, to the effect that if appealed from, the interdict need not be observed; the efforts made by city councils to force the clergy to conduct worship; all show its effectiveness. It is true that where, because of sympathy with the excommunicated princes, the clergy declared the interdict unjust, they disregarded it. Also, as in the case of Bohemia, where the churches of the heretics proved attractive, the interdict was relaxed. Yet, when the interdict was carried out, as it usually was, " the common people " missed the worship, and, when the interdict was again relaxed, they " rejoiced."

BIBLIOGRAPHY

DOCUMENTARY SOURCES

Raynaldus, O. Annales Ecclesiastici. Vol. 10-11 (Lucae, 1754, etc.).
Senckenberg, H. C. Selecta juris et historiarum (6 volumes. Frankfort, 1734-1742).
Joannis, G. C. Scriptores rerum Mogunticarum (3 volumes. Frankfort, 1723-1727).
Fontes Rerum Austriacarum. 2 Abtheilung. Diplomatia et Acta.
    Vol. 20: Urkundliche Beiträge zur Geschichte Böhmens und seiner
        Nachbarländer im Zeitalter Georgs von Podiebrad (Vienna,
        1860).
    Vol. 42: Urkunden und Aktenstücke zur österreichischen Geschichte
        im Zeitalter Kaiser Friedrichs III und König Georgs von
        Böhmen (Vienna, 1879).
    Vol. 44: Briefe und Akten zur österreichisch-deutschen Geschichte
        im Zeitalter Kaiser Friedrichs III (Vienna, 1885).
    Vol. 46: Urkundliche Nachträge zur österreichisch-deutschen Ge-
        schichte im Zeitalter Kaiser Friedrichs III. ed. A. Bachmann
        (Vienna, 1892).
Verein für Nassauische Altertumskunde und Geschichtsforschung
    Annalen (18 volumes; Wiesbaden, 1830-1891).
Jannsen, J. Frankforts Reichskorrespondenz nebst andern ver-
    wandten Aktenstücken von 1376 bis 1519. 2 Band, 1 Abtheil
    (Freiburg im Breisgau, 1865).
Archiv für österreichische Geschichte (Vienna, 1846, etc.).
Freher, M. Germanicarum rerum scriptores (3 volumes, Frankfort,
    1611-1637).
——, ed. Struve. 3 vols. 1717.
Scriptores rerum Silesiacarum. Volumes 7, 8, 9, 10 (Breslau, 1872-
    1893).
Codex diplomaticus Saxoniae Regiae (24 volumes, 1864-1909).
Müller, J. J. Des heiligen Römischen Reiches Deutscher Nation
    Reichstagstheatrum (3 Teile. Jena, 1713).
Chmel, J. Materialen zur österreichischen Geschichte (2 volumes.
    Vienna, 1837-1838).
Theiner, A. Vetera Monumenta historica Hungariam sacram illus-
    trantia vol. 2 (Rome, 1860).
Muratori, L. Rerum Italicarum scriptores (28 volumes in folio.
    Milan, 1723-1751).
    Gaspar Veronensis, Vita Pauli II, in Volume 3.
    Cronica di Bologna, in Volume 18.
    Annales Bononienses fratris Hieronymi de Barsellis, in Volume 23.
    Jacobus Vollaterranus, Diarium Romanum, in Volume 23.
    Navagiero, A., Storia della repubblica Veneziana, in Volume 23.
Monstrelet, E. de. Chroniques. Ed. Buchon, Collection des chron-
    iques nationales.
Aeneas Silvius. Opera (Basel, 1551).
Archivio della Societa Romana di storia patria (Rome, 1878–).
Tummulillis, Angelo de. Notabilia temporum. ed. Corvisieri, C.
    (Rome, 1890).

Commines, Phil. de. Ses lettres et negociations. Ed. Kerwyn de
　　Lettenhove (Brussels, 1867-1874).
Lettres de Louis XI. Ed. Vaesen and Charavay. 7 volumes (Paris,
　　1883-1900).
Lenglet du Fresnoy. Ed. Memoires de Philippe de Commines. Vol.
　　3 (London and Paris, 1747).
Nardi, Jacopo (1476-1563?). Istorie della Citta di Firenze. Ed.
　　Gelli, A. Vol. I (Florence, 1868).
Monumenta medii aevi historica res gestas Poloniae illustrantia
　　(Cracow, 1876, etc.).
Monumenta Habsburgica. I Abtheilung: Das Zeitalter Maximilians
　　I. Ed. Chmel, J. 3 volumes (Vienna, 1854-58).
Beiträge zur Vaterländischen Geschichte. 15 volumes (Basel, 1839-
　　1901).
Burchard, J. Diarium. Ed. L. Thuasne. 3 volumes (Paris, 1883-85).
Rymer, T. Foedera. 20 volumes (London, 1726-1735).
Calendar of State Papers and Manuscripts relating to English Affairs
　　Existing in the Archives and Collections of Venice and in other
　　Libraries of Northern Italy. Ed. Brown, Rawden (London,
　　1864, etc.).
Infessura, Stefano. Diario della citta di Roma. Ed. Tommasini, O.
　　(Rome, 1890).
Molinet, Jean. Chroniques. Ed. Buchon, J. A. 5 volumes (Paris,
　　1827-28).
Malipiero, Domenico. Annali veneti dal 1457 al 1500. Ed. Longo, F.
　　(Florence, 1843).
Sanuto, Marino. La spedizione di Carlo VIII in Italia. Ed. Fulin, R.
　　(Venice, 1873).
Sanuto, Marino. I Diarii (Venice, 1879–).
Corpo diplomatico Portuguez. Vol. I. Ed. Rebello da Silva, L. A.
　　(Lisbon, 1862).
Gairdner, ed. Letters and Papers of Richard III and Henry VII.
　　2 volumes (London, 1867, etc.).
Fabyan, Robert. The Chronicle of Fabian (London, 1559).
Guicciardini, Francesco. The History of Italy (10 volumes). (Eng.
　　tran. London, 1763).
Sigismondo de' Conti da Foligno. Le storie de suoi tempi dal 1475
　　al 1510. 2 volumes (Rome, 1883).
Ammirato, Scipione (1531-1601). Istorie Fiorentine (Florence, 1824-
　　1827).
Lettres de Louis XII et Cardinal George d'Amboise. Volume I
　　(Brussels, 1712).
Pastor, L. von, ed. Ungedruckte Akten zur Geschichte der Päpste.
　　Vol. I (Freiburg im Breisgau, 1904).

INDEX

Achilles, Albert, Margrave of Bradenburg, 18, 33, 35.
Alfonso, Duke of Ferrara, 76.
Anguillara, Counts of, 68, 69.
Anne, Queen of France, 61.

Basel, 20, 50-52.
Basel, University of, 51.
Bentivoglio, Giovanni, 70, 71.
Bologna, 27, 70, 71, 76.
Borgia, Cesare, 68, 70.
Breslau, 23, 29-32, 34-36.
Brixen, 12, 15-17.
Bruges, 64, 65.

Calixtus III, Pope, 13.
Carvajal, Cardinal, 23, 78-81.
Casimir, King of Poland, 33, 35.
Charles VII, King of France, 22, 54.
Charles VIII, King of France, 58-60.
Chaumont, French general, 71, 77.
Colonna, Fabrizio, 66, 68.
Corvenius, Matthias, King of Hungary, 34, 36.
Cusanus, Cardinal, 12-14, 22.

Diether, Archbishop of Mainz, 18-20, 22.

Eger, 33, 34.
Erfurt, 20.

Ferdinand, King of Naples, 52, 53.
Frederick II, Elector of Brandenburg, 18, 19.
Frederick I, Elector Palatine, 18-21.
Frejus, 56.

Heidelberg, University of, 21.
Heimberg, Gregor, 21-24.
Henry VII, King of England, 61-65.

Innocent VIII, Pope, 52, 53, 62, 64.

Leipzig, University of, 31, 32.
Louis XI, King of France, 32, 40, 42-45, 48, 55-57.

Louis XII, King of France, 61, 71, 77.

Mainz, 18-20, 22.
Malatesta, Sigismondo, Lord of Rimini, 27, 28.
Malipiero, 60.
Maximilian I, King of the Romans, and Emperor elect, 63-65, 70, 78.
Milan, 44-46, 50, 59, 80.
Moravia, 30, 34.

Nuremberg, 15, 21.

Olmütz, 25, 36.
Orsini, Virginio, 66.

Paris, University of, 61.
Paul II, Pope, 30-36, 68.
Pazzi, Conspiracy of the, 38.
Perugia, 27, 38.
Philip, Elector Palatine, 66, 67.
Philip the Fair, Archduke of Austria and King of Castile, 64, 65.
Pilsen, 30, 32.
Pisa, Council of, (1512), 77.
Pius II, Pope, 12, 14-24, 27, 28, 54.
Prague, 23, 25, 32, 34.

René, Duke of Anjou, 56.
Riario, Rafello, Cardinal, 38, 40, 41.
Reuchlin, Johann, 67.

Sanseverino, Cardinal, 79-81.
Scala, Bartholomeo, Chancellor of Florence, 40, 41.
Sigismund, Archduke of Tyrol, 12-18, 20-23, 54.
Sixtus IV, Pope, 24, 25, 37-39, 41-50, 56, 61, 75.
Suffolk, Earl of (Edmund de la Pole), 63, 64.

Tyrol, 14-18, 22.

Venice, 28, 44-46, 59, 71, 76.
Vienna, University of, 81.

Waldensians, 57, 58.
Würzburg, 21, 23.

Johns Hopkins University Studies
in Historical and Political Science

The University Studies will continue to publish, as heretofore, the results of recent investigations in History, Political Economy, and Political Science.

The titles given below are now announced; other numbers will follow from time to time.

The State as a Party Litigant. By R. D. WATKINS. $2.00.

The Relation of Thomas Jefferson to American Foreign Policy, 1783-1793. By W. K. WOOLERY. $1.00.

Ecclesiastical Censure at the End of the 15th Century. By W. K. GOTWALD. $1.00.

The Constitutional Status and Government of Alaska. By G. W. SPICER.

Press Censorship in England, 1534-1603. By C. S. SYDNOR.

The Workers' Party and American Trade Unions. By DAVID N. SCHNEIDER.

The Influence of British Labor upon Politics and Legislation, 1875-1900. By W. C. MALLALIEU.

The Legislature of Virginia: Its Organization and Procedure. By J. E. PATE.

The Virginia Constitutional Convention of 1901-1902. By R. C. MCDANEL.

The cost of subscription for the regular annual series, comprising about 600 pages, is $5.00. Single numbers, or special monographs, at special prices. Complete contents of previous volumes are given on pages viii-xii.

RECENT BOOKS ON ECONOMICS

THE THEORY OF INTERNATIONAL PRICES

By James W. Angell

"The work shows deep thought, and whatever opposition Dr. Angell's conclusions may meet, his study is a valuable addition to the literature on international price relationships."—*Bankers Magazine* (London). "A work of solid learning, worthy of the distinguished series in which it appears."—*London Times*. "The work is admirably prepared as a scholarly consideration of a most difficult subject. As an example of clear thought and sound construction it will appeal to many who have no direct interest in the material treated."—*The Independent*. $5.00 a copy.

THE FOUR KINDS OF ECONOMIC VALUE

By Correa M. Walsh

Value has been a fertile source of confusion in economic thinking. Mr. Walsh, who has long been known as an acute and competent investigator in the field of economics, declares that in the interest of precision, four kinds of value should be recognized—use-value, esteem-value, cost-value, and exchange value. In this book his task has been to discriminate between them and to show how the distinctions, if kept clearly in mind, will help in the statement and in the solution of various economic problems. $1.75 a copy.

CHAPTERS ON MACHINERY AND LABOR

By George E. Barnett

"If economists are to contribute more fully toward the solution of industrial problems, a great number of first-hand studies of factory life and conditions will need to be made. Professor Barnett has put us in his debt by publishing the results of his study of the problem—the displacement of skill by machinery. Studies were made of the introduction of the linotype, the use of the stone-planer, the introduction of the semi-automatic bottle machinery and of the automatic bottle machinery. The author then proceeds to test the conclusions of other students in the light of his own investigations. . . . It is an exceptionally good book and should be read by those interested in the labor problem."—*New York Evening Post*. $2.00 a copy.

HARVARD UNIVERSITY PRESS

44 Randall Hall, Cambridge, Mass.

A REPRINT OF ECONOMIC TRACTS

Edited by JACOB H. HOLLANDER.

Asgill, " Several Assertions Proved." London, 1696. Price, 50 cents.

Barbon, " A Discourse of Trade." London, 1690. Price, 50 cents.

Berkeley, " The Querist, containing several queries proposed to the consideration of the public." Parts I, II, III. Dublin, 1735-37. Price, $1.00.

Fauquier, " An Essay on Ways and Means of raising Money for the support of the present war, without increasing the public debts." London, 1756. Price, 50 cents.

Fortrey, " England's Interest Considered." Cambridge, 1663. Price, 50 cents.

Longe, " A Refutation of the Wage-Fund Theory." London, 1866. (Out of print.)

Malthus, " An Inquiry into the Nature and Progress of Rent." London, 1815. (Out of print.)

Massie, " An Essay on the Governing Causes of the Natural Rate of Interest; wherein the sentiments of Sir William Petty and Mr. Locke, on that head, are considered." London, 1750. Price, 50 cents.

North, " Discourses upon Trade." London, 1691. Price, 50 cents.

Ricardo, " Three Letters on ' The Price of Gold.' " London, 1809. (Out of print.)

Vanderlint, " Money answers all Things: or an essay to make money sufficiently plentiful amongst all ranks of people, and increase our foreign and domestick trade." London, 1734. Price, $1.00.

West, " Essay on the Application of Capital to Land." London, 1815 (Out of print.)

DISTURBING ELEMENTS IN THE STUDY AND TEACHING OF POLITICAL ECONOMY

By JAMES BONAR.

156 pages. 8vo. Price, $1.00.

This volume consists of five lectures delivered at the Johns Hopkins University in the spring of 1910. As the title suggests, the lectures are discourses not on economic error in general, but on the more subtle fallacies which are apt to invade the reasoning of trained economists in spite of learning and discipline. The lectures are distinguished by the scholarly tone and philosophical breadth that characterizes Dr. Bonar's writings.

AMERICAN CITIZENSHIP AND ECONOMIC WELFARE

By JACOB H. HOLLANDER.

132 pages. 16mo. $1.25.

This volume gives a frank review of the current obligations of the citizen (a) as producer, (b) as employer and (c) as taxpayer. The critical quality of the immediate economic situation is recognized, and an earnest attempt is made to point out how the ordinary citizen of the United States, animated neither by ill-balanced radicalism nor by solid resistance to change, can at this juncture of affairs and within the range of his normal activities render the largest service to his country and his fellow-men.

THE JOHNS HOPKINS PRESS,
Baltimore, Maryland

ALBERT SHAW LECTURES ON DIPLOMATIC HISTORY

THE JOHNS HOPKINS PRESS

Baltimore, Maryland

CHINA—AN ANALYSIS

By FRANK J. GOODNOW.

298 pages. 12mo. $2.00.

The author has attempted to picture Chinese life against a European background. The contrast of what have appeared to him to be the salient features of Occidental and Oriental Civilization has helped him to reach conclusions which he ventures to believe are correct with regard to the Chinese problem. It is hoped that this contrast will have the same effect in helping those who read the book in their understanding of a subject which cannot be said to be generally well understood. The volume embraces eight chapters: Physical Characteristics and Origins, Economic, Intellectual, Philosophical, Social, Political, Modern and Future China.

AMERICAN RELATIONS WITH CHINA

198 pages. Octavo. Paper, $1.00. Cloth, $1.50.

This book is a result of a unique attempt by American citizens to understand their responsibilities to China. Two hundred leaders of organizations formed themselves into a study group, engaged the help of experts, and finally came together for a conference. The fruits of this study and discussion have been brought together in a handy volume, which, with its index and bibliography of books and significant periodical articles, will prove invaluable to every one who is watching the progress of the conferences on customs autonomy and extraterritoriality at Peking.

THE INTERNATIONAL OPIUM CONFERENCES AT GENEVA:

Statements of the Chinese Delegation.

172 pages. 12mo. $1.50.

In this volume, Dr. Sao-Ke Alfred Sze who was the head of the Chinese Delegation to the two Conferences, has gathered together all the formal statements made by the Delegations and thus presents in complete, definite and authentic form the views of the Chinese Government with regard to the international problem of regulating the traffic in narcotic habit-forming drugs and controlling the production of the raw materials from which these drugs are manufactured. The statements included in the volume are grouped under appropriate topical heads, and thus enable the reader to obtain an easy comprehension of the character and scope of the general problem. Students of this problem will undoubtedly find it a great convenience to have the views and arguments of the Chinese Government thus authentically and comprehensively presented in a single and compact volume.

ADDRESSES

By His Excellency SAO-KE ALFRED SZE, LL. D.,

Chinese Minister to the United States.

142 pages. 12mo. $1.25.

This volume contains five addresses delivered to various audiences by Dr. Sze during the winter of 1925-1926. Dealing, as they do, with a frank and fundamental manner with the present political situation of China, and with the international problems arising out of that situation, these addresses cannot but be of great value to all persons interested in Far Eastern politics. The titles given to the addresses will indicate their scope and some of the topics dealt with: I. The Problem of China; II. The Causes of China's Discontent: How They May Be Removed; III. International Aspects of the Chinese Situation; IV. Extraterritoriality in China; V. China's Unequal Treaties.

THE JOHNS HOPKINS PRESS

Baltimore, Maryland

PUBLICATIONS OF THE
INSTITUTE FOR GOVERNMENT RESEARCH
WASHINGTON, D. C.

The Institute for Government Research is an association of citizens for co-operating with public officials in the scientific study of government with a view to promoting efficiency and economy in its operations and advancing the science of administration. It aims to bring into existence such information and materials as will aid in the formation of public opinion and will assist officials particularly those of the National Government, in their efforts to put the public administration upon a more efficient basis.

To this end it seeks, by the thoroughgoing study and examination of the best administrative practices, public and private, American and foreign, to formulate those principles which lie at the basis of all sound administration, and to determine their proper adaptation to the specific needs of our public administration.

STUDIES IN ADMINISTRATION.

* Out of print.

The System of Financial Administration of Great Britain. By W. F. Willoughby, W. W. Willoughby, and S. M. Lindsay. 378 pp. $3.

The Budget. By René Stourm. T. Plazinski, Translator; W. F. Mc-Caleb, Editor. 648 pp. $4.

The Canadian Budgetry System. By H. C. Villard and W. W. Willoughby. 390 pp. $3.

*The Problem of a National Budget. By W. F. Willoughby. 234 pp.

The Movement for Budgetry Reform in the States. By W. F. Willoughby. 266 pp. $3.

Teachers' Pension Systems in the United States. By Paul Studensky. 474 pp. $3.

Organized Efforts for the Improvement of Methods of Administration in the United States. By Gustavus A. Weber. 408 pp. $3.

The Federal Service: A Study of the System of Personnel Administration of the United States Government. By Lewis Mayers. 624 pp. $5.

*The Reorganization of the Administrative Branch of the National Government. By W. F. Willoughby. 314 pp.

The Development of National Administrative Organization in the United States. By L. M. Short. 532 pp. $5.

The Statistical Work of the National Government. By Laurence F. Schmeckebier. 590 pp. $5.

Manual of Accounting and Reporting for the Operating Services of the National Government. By Henry P. Seidemann. 422 pp. $5.

The National Government and Public Health. By James A. Tobey. 441 pp. $3.

The National Budget System, with Suggestions for Its Improvement. By W. F. Willoughby. 360 pp. $3.00.

The Department of Justice of the United States. By Albert Langeluttig. 334 pp. $3.00.

The Legal Status and Functions of the General Accounting Office. By W. F. Willoughby. 204 pp. $3.00.

PRINCIPLES OF ADMINISTRATION.

Principles Governing the Retirement of Public Employees. By Lewis Meriam. 508 pp. $3.

Principles of Government Purchasing. By Arthur G. Thomas. 290 pp. $3.

Principles of Government Accounting and Reporting. By Francis Oakey, C. P. A. 582 pp. $5.

Principles of Personnel Administration. By Arthur W. Proctor. 256 pp. $3.

Principles of Public Administration. By W. F. Willoughby. (In press).

SERVICE MONOGRAPHS OF THE UNITED STATES GOVERNMENT,

giving in detail the history, activities, publications, etc., of the several Administrative Federal Services.

* Sold only with complete sets.

*1. The Geological Survey. 174 pp.
*2. The Reclamation Service. 190 pp.
3. The Bureau of Mines. 174 pp. $1.
4. The Alaskan Engineering Commission. 134 pp. $1.
5. The Tariff Commission. 84 pp. $1.
6. The Federal Board for Vocational Education. 86 pp. $1.
7. The Federal Trade Commission. 92 pp. $1.
8. The Steamboat-Inspection Service. 142 pp. $1.
9. The Weather Bureau. 100 pp. $1.
10. The Public Health Service. 312 pp. $2.
11. The National Parks Service. 184 pp. $1.
12. The Employees' Compensation Commission. 98 pp. $1.
13. The General Land Office. 236 pp. $1.50.
14. The Bureau of Education. 172 pp. $1.
15. The Bureau of Navigation. 136 pp. $1.
16. The Coast and Geodetic Survey. 120 pp. $1.
17. The Federal Power Commission. 138 pp. $1.
18. The Interstate Commerce Commission. 182 pp. $1.
19. The Railroad Labor Board. 94 pp. $1.
20. The Division of Conciliation. 50 pp. $1.
21. The Children's Bureau. (In Press.)
22. The Women's Bureau. 44 pp. $1.
23. The Office of the Supervising Architect. 150 pp. $1.
24. The Bureau of Pensions. 150 pp. $1.
25. The Bureau of Internal Revenue. 284 pp. $1.50.
26. The Bureau of Public Roads. 136 pp. $1.
27. The Office of the Chief of Engineers. 178 pp. $1.
28. The U. S. Employment Service. 142 pp. $1.
29. The Bureau of Foreign and Domestic Commerce. 192 pp. $1.
30. The Bureau of Immigration. 260 pp. $1.50.
31. The Patent Office. 140 pp. $1.
32. The Office of Experiment Stations. 190 pp. $1.
33. The Customs Service. 204 pp. $1.50.
34. The Federal Farm Loan Bureau. 172 pp. $1.
35. The Bureau of Standards. 316 pp. $2.
36. The Government Printing Office. 156 pp. $1.
37. The Bureau of the Mint. 102 pp. $1.
38. The Office of the Comptroller of the Currency. 96 pp. $1.
39. The Naval Observatory. 114 pp. $1.
40. The Lighthouse Service. 170 pp. $1.
42. The Hydrographic Office. 124 pp. $1.
43. The Bureau of Naturalization. 120 pp. $1.
44. The Panama Canal. 430 pp. $2.50.
45. The Medical Department of the Army. 173 pp. $1.50.
46. The General Accounting Office. (In Press.)

Orders should be addressed to

THE JOHNS HOPKINS PRESS,
Baltimore, Maryland.

JOHNS HOPKINS UNIVERSITY STUDIES

IN

HISTORICAL AND POLITICAL SCIENCE

*Not sold separately.

FIRST SERIES.—1883.

(Complete volume out of print.)

I. An Introduction to American Institutional History. By E. A. FREEMAN. 25 cents.
II. The Germanic Origin of New England Towns. By H. B. ADAMS. 50 cents.
III. Local Government in Illinois. By ALBERT SHAW.—Local Government in Pennsylvania By E. R. L. GOULD. 30 cents.
IV. Saxon Tithingmen in America. By H. B. ADAMS. 50 cents.
V. Local Government in Michigan and the Northwest. By E. W. BEMIS. 25 cents.
VI. Parish Institutions of Maryland. By EDWARD INGLE. 40 cents.
*VII. Old Maryland Manors. By JOHN HEMSLEY JOHNSON.
VIII. Norman Constables in America. By H. B. ADAMS. 50 cents.
IX-X. Village Communities of Cape Ann and Salem. By H. B. ADAMS. 50 cents.
XI. The Genesis of a New England State. By A. JOHNSTON. 30 cents.
*XII. Local Government and Schools in South Carolina. By B. J. RAMAGE.

SECOND SERIES.—1884.

(Volume sold only with complete set.)

*I-II. Methods of Historical Study. By H. B. ADAMS.
III. The Past and Present of Political Economy. By R. T. ELY. 35 cents.
IV. Samuel Adams, the Man of the Town Meeting. By JAMES K. HOSMER. 35 cents.
V-VI. Taxation in the United States. By HENRY CARTER ADAMS. 50 cents.
VII. Institutional Beginnings in a Western State. By JESSE MACY. 25 cents.
VIII-I__. ___an Money in New England, etc. By WILLIAM B. WEEDEN. 50 cents.
*X. Town and County Government in the Colonies. By E. CHANNING.
*XI. Rudimentary Society among Boys. By J. HEMSLEY JOHNSON.
XII. Land Laws of Mining Districts. By C. H. SHINN. 50 cents.

THIRD SERIES.—1885.—$4.00.

I. Maryland's Influence upon Land Cessions to the U. S. By H. B. ADAMS. 75 cents.
II-III. Virginia Local Institutions. By E. INGLE. 75 cents.
IV. Recent American Socialism. By RICHARD T. ELY. 50 cents.
V-VI-VII. Maryland Local Institutions. By LEWIS W. WILHELM. $1.00.
VIII. Influence of the Proprietors in Founding New Jersey. By A. SCOTT. 25 cents.
IX-X. American Constitutions. By HORACE DAVIS. 50 cents.
XI-XII. The City of Washington. By J. A. PORTER. 50 cents.

FOURTH SERIES.—1886.—$4.00.

(Complete volume out of print.)

*I. Dutch Village Communities on the Hudson River. By I. ELTING.
II-III. Town Government in Rhode Island. By W. E. FOSTER.—The Narragansett Planters. By EDWARD CHANNING. 50 cents.
IV. Pennsylvania Boroughs. By WILLIAM P. HOLCOMB. 50 cents.
V. Introduction to Constitutional History of the States. By J. F. JAMESON. 50 cents.
VI. The Puritan Colony at Annapolis, Maryland. By D. R. RANDALL. 50 cents.
*VII-VIII-IX. The Land Question in the United States. By S. SATO.
X. Town and City Government of New Haven. By C. H. LEVERMORE. 50 cents.
XI-XII. Land System of the New England Colonies. By M. EGLESTON. 50 cents.

FIFTH SERIES.—1887.—$4.00.

I-II. City Government of Philadelphia. By E. P. ALLINSON and B. PENROSE. 50 cents.
III. City Government of Boston. By JAMES M. BUGBEE. 25 cents.
*IV. City Government of St. Louis. By MARSHALL S. SNOW.
V-VI. Local Government in Canada. By JOHN GEORGE BOURINOT. 50 cents.
VII. Effect of the War of 1812 upon the American Union. By N. M. BUTLER. 25 cents.
VIII. Notes on the Literature of Charities. By HERBERT B. ADAMS. 25 cents.
*IX. Predictions of Hamilton and De Tocqueville. By JAMES BRYCE.
X. The Study of History in England and Scotland. By P. FREDERICQ. 25 cents.
XI. Seminary Libraries and University Extension. By H. B. ADAMS. 25 cents.
*XII. European Schools of History and Politics. By A. D. WHITE.

SIXTH SERIES.—1888.—$4.00.

(Volume sold only with complete set.)

The History of Co-operation in the United States.

SEVENTH SERIES.—1889.

(Complete volume out of print.)

I. Arnold Toynbee. By F. C. MONTAGUE. 50 cents.
II-III. Municipal Government in San Francisco. By BERNARD MOSES. 50 cents.
IV. Municipal History of New Orleans. By WM. W. HOWE. 25 cents.

*V–VI. English Culture in Virginia. By WILLIAM P. TRENT.
VII–VIII–IX. The River Towns of Connecticut. By CHARLES M. ANDREWS. $1.00.
*X–XI–XII. Federal Government in Canada. By JOHN G. BOURINOT.

EIGHTH SERIES.—1890.

(Complete volume out of print.)

I–II. The Beginnings of American Nationality. By A. W. SMALL. $1.00.
III. Local Government in Wisconsin. By D. E. SPENCER. 25 cents.
*IV. Spanish Colonization in the Southwest. By F. W. BLACKMAR.
V–VI. The Study of History in Germany and France. By P. FREDERICQ. $1.00.
VII–IX. Progress of the Colored People of Maryland. By J. R. BRACKETT. $1.00.
*X. The Study of History in Belgium and Holland. By P. FREDERICQ.
XI–XII. Seminary Notes on Historical Literature. By H. B. ADAMS and others. 50 cents.

NINTH SERIES.—1891.

(Volume sold only with complete set.)

*I–II. Government of the United States. By W. W. WILLOUGHBY and W. F. WILLOUGHBY.
III–IV. University Education in Maryland. By B. C. STEINER.—The Johns Hopkins University (1876–1891). By D. C. GILMAN. 50 cents.
*V–VI. Municipal Unity in the Lombard Communes. By W. K. WILLIAMS.
VII–VIII. Public Lands of the Roman Republic. By A. STEPHENSON. 75 cents.
*IX. Constitutional Development of Japan. By T. IYENAGA.
*X. A History of Liberia. By J. H. T. McPHERSON.
XI–XII. The Indian Trade in Wisconsin. By F. J. TURNER. 50 cents.

TENTH SERIES.—1892.—$4.00.

I. The Bishop Hill Colony. By MICHAEL A. MIKKELSEN. 50 cents.
II–III. Church and State in New England. By PAUL E. LAUER. 50 cents.
IV. Church and State in Maryland. By GEORGE PETRIE. 50 cents.
V–VI. Religious Development of North Carolina. By S. B. WEEKS. 50 cents.
VII. Maryland's Attitude in the Struggle for Canada. By J. W. BLACK. 50 cents.
VIII–IX. The Quakers in Pennsylvania. By A. C. APPLEGARTH. 75 cents.
X–XI. Columbus and his Discovery of America. By H. B. ADAMS and H. WOOD. 50 cts.
XII. Causes of the American Revolution. By J. A. WOODBURN. 50 cents.

ELEVENTH SERIES.—1893.—$4.00.

I. The Social Condition of Labor. By E. R. L. GOULD. 50 cents.
II. The World's Representative Assemblies of To-Day. By E. K. ALDEN. 50 cents.
III–IV. The Negro in the District of Columbia. By EDWARD INGLE. $1.00.
V–VI. Church and State in North Carolina. By STEPHEN B. WEEKS. 50 cents.
VII–VIII. The Condition of the Western Farmer, etc. By A. F. BENTLEY. $1.00.
IX–X. History of Slavery in Connecticut. By BERNARD C. STEINER. 75 cents.
XI–XII. Local Government in the South. By E. W. BEMIS and others. $1.00.

TWELFTH SERIES.—1894.—$4.00.

I–II. The Cincinnati Southern Railway. By J. H. HOLLANDER. $1.00.
III. Constitutional Beginnings of North Carolina. By J. S. BASSETT. 50 cents.
IV. Struggle of Dissenters for Toleration in Virginia. By H. R. McILWAINE. 50 cents.
*V–VI–VII. The Carolina Pirates and Colonial Commerce. By S. C. HUGHSON.
VIII–IX. Representation and Suffrage in Massachusetts. By G. H. HAYNES. 50 cents.
X. English Institutions and the American Indian. By J. A. JAMES. 25 cents.
XI–XII. International Beginnings of the Congo Free State. By J. S. REEVES. 50 cents.

THIRTEENTH SERIES.—1895.—$4.00.

I–II. Government of the Colony of South Carolina. By E. L. WHITNEY. 75 cents.
III–IV. Early Relations of Maryland and Virginia. By J. H. LATANÉ. 50 cents.
V. The Rise of the Bicameral System in America. By T. F. MORAN. 50 cents.
VI–VII. White Servitude in the Colony of Virginia. By J. C. BALLAGH. 50 cents
VIII. The Genesis of California's First Constitution. By R. D. HUNT. 50 cents.
IX. Benjamin Franklin as an Economist. By W. A. WETZEL. 50 cents.
X. The Provisional Government of Maryland. By J. A. SILVER. 50 cents.
XI–XII. Government and Religion of the Virginia Indians. By S. R. HENDREN. 50 cents.

FOURTEENTH SERIES.—1896.—$4.00.

I. Constitutional History of Hawaii. By HENRY E. CHAMBERS. 25 cents.
II. City Government of Baltimore. By THADDEUS P. THOMAS. 25 cents.
III. Colonial Origins of New England Senates. By F. L. RILEY. 50 cents.
IV–V. Servitude in the Colony of North Carolina. By J. S. BASSETT. 50 cents.
VI–VII. Representation in Virginia. By J. A. C. CHANDLER. 50 cents.
VIII. History of Taxation in Connecticut (1636-1776). By F. R. JONES. 50 cents.
IX–X. A Study of Slavery in New Jersey. By HENRY S. COOLEY. 50 cents.
XI–XII. Causes of the Maryland Revolution of 1689. By F. E. SPARKS. 50 cents.

FIFTEENTH SERIES.—1897.—$4.00.

I–II. The Tobacco Industry in Virginia since 1860. By B. W. ARNOLD. 50 cents.
III–V. Street Railway Systems of Philadelphia. By F. W. SPEIRS. 75 cents.
VI. Daniel Raymond. By C. P. NEILL. 50 cents.

ix

THIRTY-FOURTH SERIES.—1916.—$4.00.

(Complete in four numbers.)

I. The Boycott in American Trade Unions. By LEO WOLMAN. $1.00.
II. The Postal Power of Congress. By LINDSAY ROGERS. $1.00.
III. Control of Strikes in American Trade Unions. By G. M. JANES.
IV. State Administration in Maryland. By JOHN L. DONALDSON. $1.00 ; cloth $1.25.

THIRTY-FIFTH SERIES.—1917.—$4.00.

(Complete in three numbers.)

I. Virginia Committee System and American Revolution. By J. M. LEAKE. $1.00; cloth $1.25.
II. The Organizability of Labor. By W. O. WEYFORTH. $1.50.
III. Party Organization and Machinery in Michigan. By A. C. MILLSPAUGH. $1.00 ; clo. $1.25.

THIRTY-SIXTH SERIES.—1918.—$4.00.

(Complete in four numbers.)

I. The Standard of Living in Japan. By K. MORIMOTO. $1.25.
II. Sumptuary Law in Nurnberg. By K. R. GREENFIELD. $1.25; cloth $1.50.
III. The Privileges and Immunities of State Citizenship. By R. HOWELL. $1.00 ; cloth $1.25.
IV. French Protestantism, 1559–1562. By C. G. KELLY. $1.25 ; cloth $1.50.

THIRTY-SEVENTH SERIES.—1919.—$4.25.

(Complete in four numbers.)

I. Unemployment and American Trade Unions. By D. P. SMELSER, JR. $1.25.
II. The Labor Law of Maryland. By M. H. LAUCHHEIMER. $1.25 ; cloth $1.50.
III. The American Colonization Society, 1817-1840. By E. L. FOX. $2.00 ; cloth $2.25.
IV. The Obligation of Contracts Clause of the United States Constitution. By W. B. HUNTING. $1.00 ; cloth $1.25.

THIRTY-EIGHTH SERIES.—1920.—$4.25.

(Complete in three numbers.)

I. The United States Department of Agriculture. By W. L. WANLASS. $1.25; cloth $1.75.
II. The Amalgamated Association of Iron, Steel and Tin Workers. By J. S. ROBINSON. $1.50 ; cloth $2.00.
III. Employment of Plebiscite in the Determination of Sovereignty. By J. MATTERN. $1.50.

THIRTY-NINTH SERIES.—1921.—$5.75.

(Complete in three numbers.)

I. The Capitalization of Goodwill. By KEMPER SIMPSON. $1.00.
II. The Rise of the Cotton Mills in the South. By BROADUS MITCHELL. $2.50.
III. The International Molders' Union of North America. By FRANK T. STOCKTON. $1.50.

FORTIETH SERIES.—1922.—$5.75.

(Complete in four numbers.)

I. The Presidential Campaign of 1832. By SAMUEL R. GAMMON, JR. $1.50.
II. The Canadian Reciprocity Treaty of 1854. By C. C. TANSILL. $1.00.
III. Recent Problems in Admiralty Jurisdiction. By EDGAR T. FELL. $1.25.
IV. The Creation of the Presidency, 1775-1789: A Study in Constitutional History. By CHARLES C. THACH, JR. $1.50.

FORTY-FIRST SERIES.—1923.—$5.75.

(Complete in four numbers.)

I. Paper Money in Maryland, 1727–1789. By KATHRYN L. BEHRENS. $1.00.
II. The Shop Committee in the United States. By CARROLL E. FRENCH. $1.25.
III. Bavaria and the Reich: The Conflict over the Law for the Protection of the Republic. By J. MATTERN. $1.25.
IV. James Henry Hammond, 1807-1864. By ELIZABETH MERRITT. $1.50.

FORTY-SECOND SERIES.—1924.—$5.75.

(Complete in four numbers.)

I. Contemporary French Opinion on the American Civil War. By W. REED WEST. $1.50.
II. Frederick Law Olmsted: a Critic of the Old South. By BROADUS MITCHELL. $1.50.
III. Constitutional Doctrines of Oliver Wendell Holmes. By DORSEY RICHARDSON. $1.50.
IV. Reformation in Poland: Some Social and Economic Aspects. By PAUL FOX. $1.50.

FORTY-THIRD SERIES.—1925.—$5.75.

(Complete in three numbers.)

I. The Agrarian Movement in North Dakota. By PAUL R. FOSSUM. $1.75.
II. The Virginia Frontier, 1754-1763. By LOUIS K. KOONTZ. $1.50.
III. The Ordinance Making Powers of the President of the United States. By JAMES HART. $2.50.

FORTY-FOURTH SERIES.—1926.—$5.75.

I. Sumptuary Legislation and Personal Regulation in England. By F. ELIZABETH BALDWIN. $2.50 ; cloth, $3.00.
II. The Doctrine of Continuous Voyage. By H. W. BRIGGS. $2.00 ; cloth, $2.50.
III. The Wage Policies of Labor Organizations in a Period of Industrial Depression. By V. J. WYCKOFF. $1.00.

The set of forty-four series of Studies is offered (except volumes one, four, seven and eight) uniformly bound in cloth, for library use for $171.00 net. The separate volumes may be had bound in cloth at the prices stated.